BUILDING CONSTRUCTION PEOPLE
BOOK 1

BUILDING PEOPLE WHO BUILD HOSPITALS

A NEW PLAN FOR HEALTHCARE CONSTRUCTION

MICHAEL TOFTELY

ISBN:
979-8-9952142-0-5 (Hardcover)
979-8-9952142-1-2 (Paperback)
979-8-9952142-2-9 (eBook — Kindle)
979-8-9952142-3-6 (Audiobook)

Contents

Get Your Free Gift: The CM's Toolkit

To put the principles in this book into practice, I've compiled the CM's Toolkit — a collection of checklists, templates, and practical tools built specifically for healthcare construction project managers.

These are the same tools I reach for on real projects. They cover everything from daily job site management to critical system shutdowns to contract review. No fluff — just the meat and potatoes of daily project management.

Download your free copy at:
buildingconstructionpeople.com

THE SECOND HALF

Why This Book Needed to Be Written

The first time a superintendent took me out to lunch, I knew I was onto something.

It wasn't because I was some kind of construction genius—trust me, I was not. I was maybe three years out of college, still learning the difference between a change order and a field directive, and asking enough questions to drive everyone around me half-crazy. But Marcus, a veteran Texas super who wore his UT Longhorns gear like a uniform, looked me in the eye over sushi and said something that stuck: "Toftely, that MRI project went perfect. Your attention to the small stuff made this whole thing work."

That project was an outpatient MRI building at a Southern California hospital. Nothing glamorous—just a small addition to a bigger tower expansion. But for me, it was where I learned that doing simple things consistently can make you valuable in a business where most people are too busy fighting fires to even think about preventing them.

Here's what I did that was so revolutionary: I walked the job every day at 6:30 AM, breakfast burrito in hand, worked through RFIs—requests for information, the lifeblood of construction communication—with a foreman named Keith who became an unlikely mentor, and made sure the billing matched what actually got done each month. Groundbreaking stuff, right?

Here's the thing—it worked. Everything arrived on time. We stayed on budget. That 6,000-pound MRI machine got into the building without a hitch, thanks to long hours figuring out the logistics. I became my company's so-called "MRI expert," not because I knew anything special about magnetic resonance imaging, but because I'd figured out that the small, boring, daily discipline of paying attention was the real secret sauce.

I was building what would become the foundation of my entire career philosophy, even though I didn't know it yet.

The Winding Road to Lunch

See, my path to that sushi restaurant wasn't exactly a straight line.

I had started college at Montana State University, but the ski slopes took priority over attending classes. When my grades reflected that choice, I dropped out to live "the Montana life." My father—a contractor who owned a commercial drywall and plaster company—wasn't having it. He valued hard work, and seeing his son drift without purpose didn't sit well. "You're on your own," he told me, cutting off financial support.

So there I was, a young twenty-something, working as a ski patroller and framing carpenter, before bouncing around California, New Zealand, and Australia for a year. When I returned to Montana, I found myself carrying drywall through snow drifts in the dead of winter on a spec home job. Struggling through those drifts with heavy sheets, I told myself, "I'm sure I can do better than this." That's when something clicked.

I enrolled in technical college in Minneapolis the next day.

From that moment, my mindset completely shifted. I became motivated and laser-focused. I earned a grant to cover my second year and later won a coveted internship with one of Minnesota's largest general contractors. That internship got me to California, working for a smaller outfit building multifamily housing in Orange County. The company's leadership was, let's say, limited. There was one project manager, an absentee owner, and me trying to figure out how not to screw things up. It was sink or swim, and I chose to swim.

From there, I moved to a large national subcontracting company where I got my first taste of hospital work. Two years on a women's patient tower with labor and delivery floors taught me that healthcare construction wasn't just about putting up another building—it was about building spaces where patients would receive top-level care by their entrusted doctors, our clients. In a distant way, I was proud of being a part of it.

It was at that Southern California hospital with Marcus and Keith, though, where the foundation really took shape. Keith would show up at my office every night with a stack of RFIs. Instead of just dropping them off and leaving, he'd take the time to explain each one, helping me understand what he was really asking for and why it mattered. I became his inside man for getting answers fast, and he became my real-world teacher for understanding how buildings actually get built.

It was a partnership that worked because we both got what we needed. He needed quick answers to keep his crew moving. I needed to learn my trade from someone who was an absolute expert. The result? The exterior skin went up on schedule and on budget, and that little MRI building became a perfect example of what happens when you focus on the entire process instead of just the outcome.

When Marcus took me to that lunch and validated what I'd been doing, I thought I had it all figured out. I thought I'd cracked the code for success in this business.

I was wrong.

The Wake-Up Calls I Ignored

I figured out how to be successful in the traditional sense—how to deliver projects on time and on budget, how to climb the ladder, how to build a career that looked impressive on paper. I hadn't learned the difference between success and significance. I hadn't learned that there's a cost to the relentless grind, and that cost isn't always worth paying.

The construction industry has a way of rewarding that grind. We celebrate the project manager who works weekends and answers emails at midnight. We promote the superintendent who hasn't taken a real vacation in five years. We build a culture that treats burnout as a badge of honor and mistakes exhaustion for dedication.

I bought into all of it. I wore my 60-hour weeks like a badge of honor and convinced myself that this was just what I had to do to succeed in a tough business.

Over the next 15 years, the wake-up calls came in stages, and I ignored most of them.

I got married when I was 30 years old, and was already divorced just 5 years later. I was building state-of-the-art hospitals, but couldn't build a stable life at home. I'd come back from 12-hour days too exhausted to be present. I'd miss dinners, conversations, those small moments that actually hold a relationship together. When she finally said enough, I told myself it was just the cost of building something significant. I'd figure out balance later, once I'd achieved enough, once I'd proven myself, and once I'd arrived at some imaginary finish line where the pressure would ease up.

That finish line just kept moving.

I adjusted after the divorce, kept grinding, and convinced myself that I just needed to work smarter, not necessarily any differently. The problem, I told myself, wasn't the long hours or my dedicated approach—it was that I hadn't found the right partner who understood what it took to succeed in this business.

More wake-up calls followed. I contracted walking pneumonia during a critical project, but I pushed through because "the project needed me." I felt exhaustion so deep that sleep didn't touch it. My relationships with family and friends slowly eroded away from neglect.

The warning sign I couldn't ignore came later, in 2025, when a ruptured appendix turned into life-threatening sepsis. I spent over a month in one of those hospitals I'd spent my career building, fighting an infection that nearly killed me.

Lying in that hospital bed, I had plenty of time to think about what really mattered.

It's one thing to read about work-life balance in a business book. It's another thing entirely to face your own mortality and realize that all those 60-hour weeks and "critical" projects won't mean much to you if you're not around to see the impact. It's a humbling feeling to realize the buildings will get built whether you destroy yourself or not. The companies will hire someone else, the projects will continue, and the industry that consumed you will just move on to the next person in line.

Your family won't just move on to the next person in line. Your health won't magically reset. The things you sacrificed for unsustainable success don't come back.

Discovering the Second Half

That's when I discovered Bob Buford's book *Halftime*, and things started to make sense.

Buford describes a transition point that many successful people face—moving from what he calls the "First Half" of life to the "Second Half." The First Half is about success: climbing the ladder, building a reputation, achieving recognition, proving yourself. It's about accumulating—more projects, more responsibility, more money, more status.

The Second Half is about significance: using what you've learned to make a real difference, developing others instead of just achieving personal goals, building something that outlasts any job .

I wasn't having a career crisis. I was at a natural transition point, and I had a choice: keep operating in First Half mode until it destroyed me, or consciously choose to build a Second Half career focused on significance.

With the help of mentors who'd walked this path before me—men like Tim and Matt at one of California's most prestigious academic medical centers, and my stepfather Les who'd modeled Second Half leadership his entire career—I started to see a different way forward.

I began to understand that the principles I'd stumbled onto early in my career weren't just about building better projects. They were about building a better way of working—a sustainable approach that could deliver exceptional results without demanding everything in return.

What This Book Offers You

This book is about finding a different path—one where you can build a helluva career without sacrificing everything that makes life worth living.

This belief is built on the same foundation I accidentally discovered at that Southern California hospital: that small, consistent actions compound into extraordinary results. But it goes deeper than that. It's also about shifting from a transactional mindset to a transformational one, from focusing solely on outcomes to nurturing the processes and people that create those outcomes.

Here's what you're going to learn:

The Foundation of Partnership (Chapter 1): How to shift from being a contractor who just delivers what's on the plans to a partner who helps solve real problems. This is where most people get it wrong—they think expertise means having all the answers, when real expertise means asking the right questions first.

The Currency of Trust (Chapter 2): How to build and maintain the only currency that actually matters on a job site. Trust isn't built through perfection—it's built through transparency, consistency, and keeping small promises every single day.

Growing Your Team (Chapter 3): How to assemble and develop a crew of hardworking, humble people united by a common mission rather than just motivated by paychecks. You'll learn why character beats credentials every time, and how to create the kind of team that handles challenges without you hovering over every decision.

Building External Partnerships (Chapter 4): How to extend that team philosophy beyond your direct reports to include architects, engineers, and contractors. The best projects happen when there are no "sides"—just one team solving problems together.

The Rhythm of Excellence (Chapter 5): How to build a sustainable career that delivers exceptional results without grinding you into dust. This is where I share the mistakes that cost me a marriage and nearly cost me my life, and what I learned about protecting what matters, while still doing great work.

Leading Through Crisis (Chapter 6): What to do when, despite your best efforts, something goes terribly wrong. I'll walk you through a crisis that could have ended my career and show you exactly how we rebuilt trust stronger than before.

Essential Skills for Daily Success (Chapter 7): The nuts-and-bolts skills that make everything else possible—from planning shutdowns in occupied hospitals, to reviewing change orders, to running meetings that actually add value.

Scaling Your Approach (Chapter 8): How to multiply your impact beyond what you can personally touch. This is about building systems that work without you, developing leaders who can carry these principles forward, and creating a legacy that outlasts any building.

Your Next Steps (Chapter 9): Where you are in your own journey from First Half to Second Half, and the specific actions you can take starting Monday morning to begin building something that lasts.

Who This Book Is For

If you're reading this, chances are you're where I was—successful by the traditional metrics but wondering if there's a better way. Maybe you're grinding through the long hours and mounting pressure, building a career that looks good from the outside while feeling increasingly hollow on the inside. Maybe you've had your own wake-up call—divorce, health scare, total burnout—or maybe you're smart enough to change course before you need one.

This book is for the project manager who wants to lead projects without sacrificing their health and family.

It's for the superintendent who's tired of the adversarial relationships and wants to build something more collaborative.

It's for the hospital leader who knows there has to be a better way to manage construction in occupied facilities.

It's for the young engineer who's watching older colleagues burn out and wants a different path.

It's for anyone who builds the places where lives are saved and wants to do it in a way that doesn't destroy their own life in the process.

What This Book Won't Do

Let me be clear about what this book isn't.

It's not a magic solution to all the challenges of healthcare construction. It won't make the work easy, and it won't eliminate the pressure or complexity of building in occupied hospitals. Healthcare construction will always be demanding. The stakes will always be high. The coordination will always be complex.

What this book will do is show you how to navigate those challenges with integrity, build teams that can weather any storm, and create a career that's sustainable not just for the next project, but for the long haul.

This book won't give you shortcuts or tricks. It will give you principles that work when applied consistently, even when—especially when—they're not convenient.

It won't make you a hero who saves every project through personal sacrifice. It will show you how to build systems and develop people so heroics become unnecessary.

The Choice You'll Make a Thousand Times

The choice between First Half thinking and Second Half leadership isn't one big decision. It's a thousand small choices you'll make in ordinary moments that don't feel significant when they happen:

- How you respond to that late-night crisis call.
- How you handle the subcontractor who's falling behind.
- How you communicate bad news to a client.
- How you treat the newest member of your team.
- Whether you work through the weekend or protect time with your family.
- Whether you hoard knowledge or transfer it.
- Whether you build dependency or build capability.

Each choice is a brick in the foundation of the type of leader you're becoming. The question is: what kind of foundation are you building?

That MRI building I worked on with Marcus is still standing, still serving patients. But what I'm most proud of isn't the building—it's that the principles I learned there became the foundation for developing dozens of other leaders, for improving how entire programs approach healthcare construction, and for creating standards that protect patients and the people who build for them.

The buildings you work on will eventually be torn down or renovated beyond recognition. The people you develop, the trust you build, the standards you establish, and the culture you create—that's the foundation that will outlast any structure.

Let's build that foundation together.

CHAPTER 1

THE FOUNDATION

From Transactional Contractor to Transformational Partner

Let me tell you about the project that taught me the difference between building a building and building a partnership.

It was an outpatient MRI facility at a Southern California hospital—nothing glamorous, just a small addition to a bigger tower expansion. But for me, a young project engineer barely three years out of college, it might as well have been the space station. This was my chance to prove I could handle something on my own, just me and Marcus, a tough Texas super who wore his UT Longhorns gear like a uniform.

I didn't want to screw it up.

I did what any ambitious young PE would do—I came up with a routine that made sense to me. Every morning at 6:30, I'd start at the food truck that had negotiated a sweet deal with the superintendents. Free food for the General Contractor staff in exchange for access to sell to the 200-plus workers on site. I'd inhale my breakfast burrito while looking at my calendar, then take a long walk around the jobsite.

I thought I was checking on progress. I was actually building relationships and trust with workers who could make or break my day—even if I didn't know it at the time. We'd talk about last night's game, commiserate about the weather, and gradually, they'd start giving me the heads-up when something wasn't quite right.

After I finished my daily inspection of the jobsite, then came the tedious part: submittals and RFIs. I hated reviewing submittals—mind-numbing paperwork that could delay critical materials if I didn't get through it quickly. As my superintendent bosses made clear, being slow on submittals would "fuck everything up," and I definitely didn't want to be that guy.

But RFIs were different. Thanks to Keith, the foreman who'd become my mentor on the project's exterior skin work, I'd learned that RFIs were like puzzles waiting to be solved. Instead of just processing them from my desk, I'd grab the relevant RFIs and head out to the job. I wanted to put my eyes on the actual problem.

That's when Marcus would see me walking around with papers in hand, and he'd give me that look.

"What are you doing now, Toftely?"

I'd explain about the RFIs, the urgency of getting answers, and how I was trying to understand the problem so we could get fast responses from the architect or engineer. Marcus, being a man of few words, would just smile without even looking at me and say, "Good."

That simple "good" meant everything. It meant I was doing something right, even if I couldn't articulate exactly what that was.

The routine worked. When we hit a snag with RF shielding design and the subcontractor was nowhere to be found—the kind of sub who worked on their own timeline regardless of your project's urgency—I kicked it up a gear. I talked to engineers, made calls to vendors, and stayed persistent until I understood the problem well enough to get the answer we needed. I did their hustling for them because the project mattered more than who got credit.

Over time, Marcus came to respect this approach. He'd even defend me when situations warranted it. At that lunch over sushi—still one of the best performance reviews I ever got—he told me the MRI project went perfectly. Everything arrived on time, the subs were well-coordinated, and even the delivery of the 6,000-pound MRI machine itself was a success, thanks to long hours figuring out how to get it into the building. You can't exactly wheel those things in.

The real validation came when I was shipped off to another project that wasn't going well, tasked with teaching my routine to project engineers on an underperforming job. That's where I met Bob, one of my favorite superintendents ever. Bob treated meeting time as nap time because he already knew how things would turn out, so why bother paying attention?

After I'd impressed Bob with my approach and helped him solve a few problems, he gave me what remains my favorite compliment ever. He managed a small smile and told me I was "handier than a pocket on a shirt."

High praise from a man who didn't waste words.

I thought I was just developing my own project management routine, but I realized much later that I had been learning the fundamental principles that separate transactional contractors from transformational partners. This routine began on a small MRI project, but it proved to be the foundation for everything that came after— for the complex hospital programs I'd eventually lead, the teams I'd develop, and the approach to healthcare construction that would define my career.

Let me break down what was actually happening in that morning routine, because these principles work whether you're managing a small MRI building or a billion-dollar hospital expansion.

Building Excellence One Choice at a Time

The difference between a good project and a great one isn't some brilliant strategy or heroic gesture. It's the accumulation of countless small, correct decisions made in the field when no one important is watching.

Years later, I witnessed this principle in action on one of the most challenging projects of my career—a Cyberknife radiation oncology installation at a major Bay Area medical center. The equipment manufacturer made my client an offer they couldn't refuse: finish the project in the next four months before the end of their fiscal year, and they'd throw in a $1 million upgrade for free.

Four months, for a project that was already pushing the limits of what seemed possible?

The design team, contractor, facility managers, and I came up with policies to expedite just about every aspect of the project. It was all hands on deck, and there were plenty of doubters who said we couldn't pull it off. But there was a foreman and a superintendent whose dedication inspired the entire team. These guys worked multiple shifts for days in a row because they understood something crucial: each shift had to be carefully handed off to the next for continuity of the work.

They couldn't just show up, do their eight hours, and go home. That project demanded a level of care and attention that defied job descriptions. They made countless small decisions that individually seemed minor—how to sequence the work, which crew should handle the handoff, when to push through and when to pause for quality— but collectively determined whether we'd make that deadline.

We finished two weeks early.

That's the power of building excellence one choice at a time. Forget the grand vision for a moment and focus on the daily work. A great project is the accumulation of countless small, unglamorous, ultimately correct decisions made in the field when no one important is watching.

It's the foreman who spends an extra hour on infection control because he knows vulnerable patients are nearby. It's the project manager who stays late to help a drowning PE catch up on their workload. It's the superintendent who takes the time to explain the "why" behind a procedure, instead of just barking orders.

Each of these moments is a crossroads. Do you choose the easy path or the right one? Do you do the minimum required, or do you treat each small choice as a brick in the project's foundation?

The Cyberknife project succeeded because a team of people consistently chose excellence when they could have chosen convenience. They understood that great results are built one small, correct decision at a time.

The Ledger of Trust: Where Every Small Promise Is Recorded

Trust is a balance you build through countless small transactions. Think of it like a bank ledger where every action is either a deposit or a withdrawal. The sum total of these transactions determines whether you have the trust capital to weather the inevitable storms of a major project.

I learned this through years of small, consistent actions that didn't seem significant at the time but compounded into something substantial. Like maintaining perfect daily project reporting for an entire year—even when I was sick or on vacation, I made sure the reporting was handed off and submitted on time. Or transparent billing practices where I'd reverse change orders when pricing came in better than expected, even though those decisions cost me revenue.

Those decisions probably cost me thousands of dollars over the years. But they built something far more valuable: a reputation for spending their money like it was my own.

Trust is built through small, consistent actions that compound over time, whether that be through good times or badI learned this during a crisis at one of the most prestigious medical centers in California. Falling conduit pieces crashed through a ceiling, landing just feet from a hospital staff member. The only reason we survived that incident was because we'd banked enough trust deposits to absorb such a massive withdrawal. I always knew trust was important, but that incident taught me that trust can be rebuilt stronger than before, through systematic effort and genuine change, not just apologies. (We will explore that crisis more in Chapter 6.)

I've seen the other side of trust as well. I've watched as contractors destroy their relationships through pure greed. One contractor specialized in bidding on projects with incomplete documents, then change-ordering projects to death. After being burned twice by those same predatory tactics, I ensured that this contractor never worked at that hospital system again.

The ledger of trust is unforgiving. You can spend years making deposits, but make enough withdrawals driven by greed or carelessness and you'll find yourself bankrupt in the only currency that really matters.

We'll dive much deeper into building and measuring trust in Chapter 2, but for now, understand this: every promise you make, from simple things like"I'll send that email by end of day," or "I'll get you those drawings byTuesday," is a transaction in the trust ledger. The people around you are tracking your balance, whether they realize it or not.

Focus on the Tacklers, Not the End Zone

A running back who is only focused on the end zone is bound to get tackled behind the line. Great leaders get their backs to focus on following their blockers and avoiding every would-be tackler on their way to paydirt.

This goes back to that validation I felt when Marcus took me to lunch and praised my attention to detail. He wasn't celebrating the completed MRI building. He was celebrating the process—the daily walks, the persistent RFI work, the relentless attention to coordination and timing. He understood something that many leaders miss: if you take care of the process, the outcome takes care of itself.

But it works the other way too. I learned to celebrate the mundane victories of the people around me. When that foreman on the Cyberknife project worked his third straight double shift to maintain continuity, I made sure everyone knew about his dedication. When a project engineer caught a potential conflict in the drawings before it became a field problem, that became a story I told in the next team meeting.

You can't wait until the ribbon cutting to acknowledge excellence. By then, it's too late to reinforce the behaviors that created that success. This philosophy becomes especially important during long, complex projects where the finish line feels impossibly far away. Hospital construction projects can stretch for years. If your team is only motivated by the final completion, they'll burn out long before they get there.

If they find pride and purpose in the everyday grind—knowing that a well-run meeting, a perfectly organized submittal, and a clean job site are all worthy of recognition—then excellence becomes a habit instead of a rare occurrence.

The best project managers I know are masters at this. They notice the small wins and call them out immediately. They celebrate muscling past every defender on the way to the endzone. They understand that motivation doesn't come from some distant completion date—it comes from every step; seeing that your daily work matters, that someone notices when you do it right, and that the small stuff you're grinding through is actually building something significant.

Diagnose Before You Prescribe: The Art of Asking the Right Questions

I learned a valuable lesson several years later, when working as an owner's representative during large-scale shutdowns in occupied hospitals. Picture this: a contractor who only cares about cutting power to certain panels that will turn off all the equipment in the patient rooms, and doesn't consult with anyone actually working on the floor. Doctors and nurses only know that their crucial equipment plugged into the wall needs to keep working or patients could die.

The bad approach? "We're cutting power Tuesday at 6 AM. Everything will be just fine." That's the contractor who doesn't think through the ramifications of that decision for the medical staff who have to continue to treat patients even while construction is continuing. That's not being a partner. That's being a dictator.

I learned to bridge this gap with careful precision. Contractors need to know what is feasible and what is not to set realistic budgets that account for potential delays and extra workforce. Medical staff need assurance that nothing gets turned off until comprehensive mitigation plans are in place.

The principle is simple: before you propose a solution, make sure you diagnose the problem from everyone's perspective. In a hospital, that "everyone" includes people whose lives depend on getting it right. (We'll dive much deeper into shutdown planning strategies and best practices in Chapter 7.)

A shutdown in a hospital is going to be either your greatest triumph or possibly your greatest failure. There's no middle ground when patient safety is at stake. That's why the diagnostic work—understanding not just the technical requirements but the human impact—is so critical.

The contractors don't know about all the life-support equipment, monitors, and critical systems that are keeping patients alive. Things they call "thingamajigs." The medical staff has no idea why it's necessary to shut down all normal power to complete the electrical work safely. Your job as a leader is to bridge that gap with very careful precision and delicateness.

This means asking questions before making statements:

- "Help me understand what equipment can't lose power in this area."

- "What's your biggest concern about this shutdown?"

- "What would make this coordination easier for your staff?"

- "What am I missing that I should be thinking about?"

These aren't rhetorical questions. You're actually listening to learn, not just waiting for your turn to talk. The diagnostic conversation isn't a formality before you implement your predetermined solution—it's where you discover what the real solution needs to be.

Uncover the Actual Goal, Not Just the Stated Need

Here's something that happens constantly in occupied hospital settings: the medical staff will tell you it's impossible to continue operations while you close off their main corridor. That's the stated need—"We can't work with the corridor closed."

But that's not the actual goal. The actual goal is maintaining safe, efficient patient care during construction. Once you understand that, you can ask as many probing questions as you need to clearly see every hit and the possible ways to get past them, to present a plan where everybody wins.

Early in my career, I learned this lesson on a major hospital expansion in Southern California. The doctors asked the hospital board for capital expenditure because they needed expanded patient rooms, a modern cath lab, an updated ER—they weren't looking for a shiny new building for the heck of it; they wanted upgraded facilities to best treat their expanding patient population.

When you focus on their actual goal instead of the stated need, everything changes. You stop being the contractor who builds what's on the plans and become the partner who helps solve their real problems.

This requires a different kind of conversation. Instead of:

"We need to close the corridor to build the new cath lab."

You ask:

> "What's not working with the current cath lab?"

> "How is that affecting patient care or physician efficiency?"

> "What would success look like from your perspective?"

> "If we could solve this problem in a completely different way than you're imagining, what would the outcome need to be?"

These questions often reveal that the building project is a means to an end, not the end itself. Maybe they need more capacity, or better workflow, or updated technology, or recruitment advantages to attract top physicians. When you understand the true goal, you might discover that the original design isn't the best solution—or that there are additional opportunities to create value beyond just delivering the building as designed.

Walk a Mile in Their Shoes: Map Their Experience

Before you ever look at the construction documents, you need to understand the people who will use the space. This means mapping the daily journeys of the hospital's key users: the nurse who will work twelve-hour shifts, the surgeon who needs quick access between operating rooms, the anxious family member trying to find their loved one, the facility manager who has to maintain all this equipment for decades to come.

By shadowing and interviewing these people, you uncover the small, compounding frustrations that a high-level construction plan would miss. The timing of a noisy demolition might seem like just a scheduling detail, but if it coincides with patient rest hours, that's a problem worth solving.

I learned this lesson on a large renovation project at a Northern California medical center. We were planning to close a major corridor for three months to replace the ceiling. The drawings showed clear detour routes marked with signage. Easy, right?

When I walked the route with the head nurse, she showed me something the architects missed: the "detour" required pushing patient beds up a ramp, around corners, through a set of double doors, and past the cafeteria during lunch hours. What looked like a hundred-foot detour on the drawings was actually a five-minute journey that would happen dozens of times per shift.

"We can make this work," she told me, "but you need to understand it's not just inconvenient—it's going to impact patient care. When a patient codes and we need to get them to the ICU fast, those extra five minutes matter."

That conversation changed everything. We redesigned the phasing to keep a narrower section of the main corridor open throughout construction. It made our work harder and more expensive, but it was the right answer, because we understood the actual goal: maintaining safe, efficient patient care, during and after construction. The ceiling needed to be replaced for the long-term safety of the facility, but we were able to do it in a way that didn't put the care of these patients at risk for several months.

These grassroots insights—understanding which hallways are critical for emergency transport, when shift changes create the most disruption, how construction dust affects vulnerable patients—are perfect examples of focusing on the small tasks that lead to great results.

When you take time to walk in their shoes, you're showing respect for the people who will live with your decisions long after you've moved on to the next project. That respect becomes the foundation for trust and partnership.

Vague Vision vs. Tangible Victory

A goal without a measurement is just a wish. One of the most important skills you can develop is working with clients to translate their construction management vision into concrete, measurable metrics.

Instead of accepting "minimal disruption to operations," push for "limit construction noise to below 50 decibels during patient care hours."

Instead of settling for "keeping the hospital clean," define success as "maintain infection control standards with daily particle counts below baseline levels."

Instead of nodding along with "working with facility staff," establish that you're aiming for "coordinate utility shutdowns with five-day advance notice and backup systems in place."

These tangible victories do two things: they ensure everyone is following the gameplan, and they provide a clear way to validate the project's success, independent of whether the building looks impressive or wins design awards.

I learned this lesson the hard way on an early project where the client kept saying they wanted "minimal impact" on their operations. We thought we were doing great—staying on schedule, keeping things relatively clean, coordinating with staff when major work was happening.

When the project ended, the client was disappointed. The building was exactly what they wanted, but they were disappointed with the process. "Minimal impact" meant something completely different than what we'd delivered.

If we'd had that specific conversation upfront—"What does minimal impact actually mean? How can we measure it? What will success look like?"—we could have aligned expectations, and possibly adjusted our approach.

Now, I start every project with specific metrics to measure our success while on the mission. Before we finalize the schedule or break ground, we sit down with all the stakeholders and define what success looks like in specific, measurable terms.

We don't promise "good communication," we promise a "response to urgent issues within two hours."

A "clean jobsite" is great, but whose definition of clean are we using to meet that requirement? Saying "zero dust migration outside construction barriers, verified by daily air quality monitoring" gives us a tangible goal for how to maintain a clean jobsite while giving them an agreed-upon standard of expectation.

We won't promise a job will be completed "on time," we offer specifics, like "substantial completion by March 15th with all systems commissioned and staff trained."

When you can point to actual improvements in patient outcomes, staff efficiency, or operational effectiveness, you've proven that the partnership created real value beyond just delivering a building on time and on budget.

Lead with Productive Ignorance: Be the Guide, Not the Hero

Being vulnerable isn't a sign of weakness or lacking knowledge. On the contrary, if you're vulnerable enough to admit when you're wrong or don't know something, it shows character that's much more valuable than the "rockstar" know-it-all approach.

If a client sees you as someone they can confide in and trust, that's gold. I learned this lesson from Keith when he patiently taught me about EIFS systems, stucco, exterior framing, and bent plates through daily RFIs. He knew he was helping me out, but our partnership worked because I needed to learn and he needed someone who could get his RFIs answered quickly. My productive ignorance created value for both of us.

Later in my career, when I had enough clout to do so, I enjoyed asking what seemed like dumb questions in meetings. If a contractor was trying to get fancy with an RFI that I knew was going to drive up costs, I'd simply ask: "Why does that need to go there? Why can't we just build it like it's shown on the plans?"

Then I'd use the power of the pause.

In the world of construction, there's enormous pressure to project expertise and confidence at all times. I've found that the people who are most secure in their knowledge are often the ones most willing to admit what they don't know. They understand that every question is an opportunity to learn something that could prevent problems down the road.

The client isn't looking for a hero who has all the answers, even before hearing the questions. They're looking for a guide who will help them navigate unfamiliar territory. Guides ask questions, listen carefully, and admit when they need to gather more information before giving advice.

I've seen too many project managers destroy their credibility by bullshitting their way through questions they didn't know the answer to. They're so worried about looking incompetent that they make up answers, and when those answers turn out to be wrong, all trust is lost.

Compare that to the project manager who says, "That's a great question and I want to give you an accurate answer. Let me check with the structural engineer and get back to you by end of day." That person just built trust by being honest about the limits of their knowledge.

Productive ignorance means being strategic about what you don't know. When you ask a "dumb" question, you're often exposing an assumption that everyone else made, but nobody actually questioned. That's valuable.

The Power of the Pause: Listen More Than You Speak

Three out of five times, contractors couldn't muster a convincing response to those simple questions I'd ask. The pause made all the difference.

This became a useful tactic in crucial meetings. I'd listen to everyone in the room in silence. When someone would notice and ask what I thought, I'd wait a good ten seconds before answering. Sometimes I'd respond with another question—sometimes a dumb question. Then I'd let them talk for another five minutes.

That pause creates space for truth. When you're quick to fill every silence, people don't have room to think, reflect, or share the insights they might not have otherwise articulated. The pause is where real communication happens.

I learned this lesson during a particularly contentious value engineering session at a major medical center. The contractor was pushing hard for a substitution that would save them significant money but would compromise the facility's long-term maintenance goals. They had slides, data, and a slick presentation. The hospital's facilities director was skeptical but couldn't quite articulate why.

Instead of jumping in with my opinion, I just asked, "What concerns you about this approach?" Then I waited.

The silence stretched out. Fifteen seconds. Twenty. The contractor started to jump back in with more sales pitch, but I held up a hand. "Hold on. Let's hear this out."

Finally, the facilities director said, "It's just... we've tried something similar before and it failed within three years. I don't want to make that mistake again."

That was the real issue—not the technical specs, but institutional memory of a previous failure. Once that was on the table, we could have a real conversation about whether this situation was different and what additional guarantees we'd need.

The pause gave him time to articulate what he was feeling but couldn't quite explain under pressure.

In our industry, there's a cultural bias toward action. We pride ourselves on making quick decisions and keeping things moving. But sometimes the most productive thing you can do is absolutely nothing. Just wait. Let the silence stretch until it becomes uncomfortable. You'll be amazed at what people will reveal when they feel compelled to fill that space.

The pause also shows respect. It demonstrates that you value what someone has said enough to actually think about it before responding.

In a world of quick reactions and knee-jerk responses, that level of consideration stands out.

Focus on the First 5 Percent: The Goal Is Shared Understanding, Not Just a Building

The initial goal isn't to build a hospital—it's to build a shared understanding of the problems you're solving and the outcomes that will define success. . Get that right, and the building takes care of itself.

Instead of selling a massive, end-to-end solution in the first meeting, focus only on what I call the "First five percent"—the discovery and alignment phase.

I learned this approach after watching too many projects start with misaligned expectations. The hospital thought they were getting one thing, the contractor priced something else, and the design team had a third interpretation. Six months into construction, everyone's frustrated because they're working toward different definitions of success.

Now I propose a small, initial engagement where the only deliverable is a "Discovery Report" that outlines:

- The diagnosed problem (not just "we need more space" but "what specifically isn't working now")

- The co-created goals (what does success look like from every stakeholder's perspective)

- The defined metrics of success (how will we know we achieved it)

- The key constraints and requirements (budget, schedule, operational limitations)

- The identified risks and mitigation strategies

This process-driven first step ensures the foundation of the entire project is solid before the first shovel ever hits the ground.

It feels slower at first. Clients sometimes push back: "Can't we just get started? We know what we need." But I've learned that every hour spent in the First Five percent saves dozens of hours during construction, dealing with misaligned expectations and preventable conflicts.

The discovery phase is where you uncover things like:

- The department director who wasn't consulted but will need to sign off later.

- The operational requirement that didn't make it into the design criteria.

- The budget assumption that doesn't match the scope expectation.

- The schedule driver that nobody mentioned but is actually driving all decisions.

These discoveries are cheap to address during the First Five percent They're expensive—sometimes catastrophically expensive—to discover during construction.

The Foundation That Changes Everything

Looking back on that MRI building, I realize the daily routine I developed was about relationship building, problem-solving, and caring enough to understand what everyone needed to do their best work. That's how you achieve true project management efficiency.

Marcus respected that approach because I consistently showed up, cared more than expected, and made everyone else's job easier. That's the foundation of transformational partnership—making success easier for everyone around you.

The transactional contractor asks, "What do you want built, when do you need it, and what's your budget?"

The transformational partner asks: "What problems are you trying to solve, what does success look like for your mission, and how can we get there together?"

It's a small shift in language that represents a massive shift in approach. One builds buildings. The other builds trust, solves problems, and creates lasting partnerships that extend far beyond any single project.

That MRI building taught me that excellence is about being the guide who helps everyone else succeed. It's about focusing on the process, not just the outcome; breaking every tackle with intention, pride and determination. It's about understanding that the small, daily disciplines—the morning job walks, the persistent RFI detective work, the relationships built over breakfast burritos, and yes, the occasional box of bagels for the nurses or facility engineers—are what create the foundation for everything that follows.

The building was just the visible result. The real work was everything that happened before the first shovel hit the ground, and after the last worker left the site.

In the world of construction, we're trained to think about deliverables: drawings, permits, materials, reports, completed structures. But a transformational partnership is built on something different—it's built on the understanding that people aren't a means to an end, they are the end. The relationships, the trust, the shared mission, the commitment to excellence— that's the real product.

The buildings will eventually be torn down or renovated. But the relationships you develop with people, the trust you build, standards you establish, and culture you create, will outlast any structure. That's what it means to move from transactional thinking to transformational leadership.

Your Next Steps

Before we move forward, take a moment to reflect on your last significant client interaction. Were you acting as a contractor or a partner? Were you focused on delivering what they said they wanted, or did you take time to understand what they actually needed?

Here's your challenge for this week: In your next project meeting, ask one diagnostic question instead of making a statement. Instead of "We'll start the electrical rough-in Monday," try "Help me understand what's most important to keep operational while we do the electrical work."

Then practice the power of the pause. Ask the question, then stay quiet. Let them fill the silence. You might be surprised by what you learn.

Also, start your own trust ledger. For the next week, keep track of every promise you make, no matter how small. Did you say you'd send that email by the end of day? Did you commit to having drawings ready by Tuesday? Did you tell someone you'd follow up on their question?

Write them down. Then track whether you kept them. You'll quickly see how many small deposits and withdrawals you're making into that bank of trust without even thinking about it.

The foundation of transformational partnership starts with that first question, that first pause, that first small promise kept. These moments seem insignificant when they happen, but they're actually the most important work you do, because every great building—and every great career—starts with getting the foundation right.

CHAPTER 2

THE CURRENCY OF A PROJECT

How to Establish Rock Solid Trust

Many years into my career at one of California's most prestigious academic medical centers, Tim called me into his office with what I thought would be a routine check-in. Instead, he told me about his intention to retire within the year.

I was happy for him—Tim had earned a well-deserved retirement after a long successful career in healthcare construction. I figured that was the end of our conversation.

"But there's something else," he said. "I'd really like for you to start considering taking over for me when I leave."

I may have gasped. I'm not sure. I was certainly flattered and surprised that Tim saw me as his potential successor.

Flash forward a few months:r I was sitting at home one evening when Matt— the vice president in charge of planning, design, and construction for the entire healthcare system—texted me out of the blue. Matt had never texted me before.

"I'd like to talk with you," the message read.

I was immediately nervous. "Sure, Matt. We can talk tomorrow morning. Is there anything I need to prepare for?"

"No. Tomorrow morning sounds great."

That was the end of the text conversation.

I found my wife and told her, "Well, honey, tomorrow I'm either going to find out I'm fired, or Matt might want me to take over for Tim."

The conversation the next morning confirmed the latter. But the path to that moment—from outsider consultant to trusted partner to potential Director of Construction—hadn't been a straight line. It was built through countless small transactions in what I call the ledger of trust.

Let me back up and show you how that trust account was built, deposit by deposit, over several years.

How an Outsider Becomes an Insider

By the time Tim made that offer, I'd been working in healthcare construction for nearly two decades, moving through different roles as my career evolved. I'd started as a project engineer, moved up to project manager, then spent time working both for general contractors and as an independent owner's representative. Each role taught me different aspects of the business and different perspectives on what makes projects succeed or fail.

My relationship with this particular medical center began when I was working as an independent construction management consultant. I'd spent several years representing a large Bay Area hospital, and during that time I'd built a strong relationship with an architecture firm's project manager named Tom. Our relationship became what I now think of as a "trust direct deposit"—built through consistent promises made and kept over time.

When I later transitioned to working for a general contractor focused on expanding their healthcare portfolio, Tom helped arrange a meeting with Tim, who was the Director of Construction at this prestigious academic medical center. In that meeting, I didn't talk about numbers, performance metrics, or accolades. Instead, I focused on my approach to healthcare construction—how I truly wanted to understand and care about the perspectives and hardships that hospitals endure during construction projects.

I was probably the only general contractor representative trying to sell work who clearly showed he cared more about the hospital than his own employer. But it was true. Through my years in various roles—as project engineer, project manager, and owner's rep—I had developed genuine empathy for the nurses and doctors trying their best to care for patients they deeply loved while we tore down walls and made it difficult to reach those patients safely.

That conversation struck a chord with Tim. Tom confirmed after the meeting: "Tim wants you."

I wasn't ready to make the move yet, due to loyalty to my current employer. A few years later, after philosophical differences with that contractor about how to maintain relationships with healthcare partners, we parted ways. That's when I reconnected with Tim about working as a construction management consultant.

He immediately said yes.

Tim assigned me to an important project with a struggling team facing major delays. The challenge: a large pneumatic tube station was positioned exactly where a corridor was supposed to go—the P-tube relocation had apparently fallen behind. The existing team had been working together for a while and didn't necessarily agree with Tim's assessment that they needed help.

I was the outsider coming in as a consultant, not an employee.

Given the situation, I applied what had become my simple formula: discipline, routine, caring about the job, and making sure the little things added up to something great. The project finished successfully, bringing in hundreds of thousands of dollars in savings while meeting the original timeline.

Two months after that project ended, a project engineer told me something that I didn't fully appreciate at the time: "You're the only construction manager I know who took a troubled project like that and brought it in with savings and on time. That simply doesn't happen around here."

The Small Deposits That Build Big Accounts

Not all trust transactions involve crisis management. Most are built through small, consistent actions that barely register at the time, but compound into solid relationships.

Early in my career, when I was working as an owner's representative for a different hospital, I had a client who was very particular about project reporting. I typically maintained meticulous records anyway, but this client made it clear they didn't want any missed days over the course of what would be about a one-year project.

I assured them it would be done. Every day. No exceptions.

As I mentioned in the previous chapter, even when I was sick or on vacation, I made sure the reporting was handed off and submitted on time. It meant training backup personnel, creating detailed handoff procedures, and sometimes working from an airport to ensure continuity. It wasn't glamorous work—just the discipline of showing up, day after day, with the information they needed.

At the end of that project, we had a perfect record; not one missed day of detailed documentation that told the complete story of how that hospital addition came to life. This seemingly mundane task reinforced something important about the power of sticking to your word.

The real payoff wasn't the documentation—it was the trust. That client knew with absolute certainty that when I made a promise, I kept it. They didn't have to worry if they'd have the information they needed for board meetings, planning sessions, or crisis management. That trust became the foundation for everything else we accomplished together.

Additional trust deposits came through honest billing practices. Throughout my career, whether working for contractors or as a consultant, I would never bill for time that was budgeted for, but not used. I also had many change orders reversed or reduced when pricing came in better than expected due to favorable time and material tickets.

I could have billed for the full number of hours and nobody would have noticed. I could have kept orders the same, even when I managed to get a better price. Honesty and transparency build trust, and when clients know they can trust you with their money, it shows they can trust you with anything.

Here's what that looks like in practice: During my consulting years, I was managing a complex equipment replacement project at a Bay Area hospital and we'd budgeted 40 hours for coordination with the facilities team. The work went smoother than expected, taking us just 28 hours.

My invoice showed 28 hours.

The facilities director called me. "Your invoice is short. We budgeted 40 hours for this phase."

"I know," I said. "But we only needed 28. I'm not going to bill you for time I didn't use."

There was a pause. "I've been doing this for twenty years and I've never had a contractor or consultant do that."

That 12-hour discount, which would have added maybe $2,400 in additional revenue, bought me something you can't purchase: the benefit of the doubt on every difficult conversation that followed. When I had to deliver bad news about a budget overrun on a different aspect of the project, the facilities director trusted that I wasn't trying to pad my fees or cover my mistakes. He knew I'd only bill for what was necessary.

That's the compound interest of trust deposits. Each small action builds on the previous ones, creating a reserve you can draw on when you inevitably need it.

The Promise: Say It, Do It, Prove It

Trust, at its core, is a series of promises kept; the compounding power of small, consistent acts of reliability. The way to earn trust is actually rather simple: Say what you will do, do what you say, and prove what you've done.

Let me show you how this works with a project that demanded absolute precision: a Gamma Knife replacement at a major San Francisco hospital. This was during my time as an independent construction management consultant, working in the role as an owner's rep.

A Gamma Knife treats brain tumors using radioactive material. The core is so sensitive that delivery trucks couldn't cross local bridges—they had to drive all the way around the bay. Homeland Security stationed law enforcement and snipers during the offloading because the material could potentially be made into a dirty bomb.

This was serious business that required months of coordination and planning.

Say It: During those planning months, I made specific promises to stakeholders—how we'd plan the rigging route from truck to basement, protect floors and walls during the move, ensure no disruption to other hospital operations, and coordinate every inch of the move since elevators couldn't be used.

Do It: I was entrusted to oversee the high-stakes operation, ensuring everyone was where they were supposed to be and everything happened when it was supposed to happen. The project went perfectly.

Prove It: After intense projects like this, I always hold debrief meetings with owners, stakeholders, and key contractors. We close the loop on planning: report whether everything went as planned or required on-the-fly adjustments and share information that will help with future improvements. For high-stakes projects, owners need complete transparency about what actually happened versus what was planned.

When a client sees this discipline in small things, they gain confidence to trust you with big things.

This system isn't foolproof. Sometimes life interferes. At that same hospital, I was awarded another project that required a bid walk for interested contractors. On the day of the walk, one of my children became very ill. In my urgency to handle that situation, I failed to properly cancel the walk.

Multiple contractors showed up, took time out of their day to show interest in our project, and were essentially stood up by me. I felt terrible.

When I called the department leader later that day to explain what happened and express my deep remorse, they completely excused the broken promise and even offered to help in any way they could. Because of the strong trust I'd built through consistent performance on previous projects, and because they understood the nature of the emergency, the hospital leadership showed understanding and compassion.

A strong trust account built through consistently keeping your promises can absorb significant failures when they're handled with immediate honesty and genuine remorse.

Here's what this looks like in daily practice:

- **Morning:** "I'll send you that updated schedule by 2 PM today."

- **Afternoon:** Send the schedule at 1:45 PM.

- **Follow-up:** "Schedule sent as promised. Let me know if you need any clarification."

It sounds absurdly simple, but most people don't do it. They say they'll send something and then forget, or they send it three days later without acknowledging that it's late. Perhaps they send it, but never follow up to close the loop.

This isn't just about keeping promises—it's about creating a standard of reliability that people can count on. When you consistently say what you'll do, do what you say, and prove you did it, people stop worrying about whether you'll follow through. Rather than being consumed with doubt, their energy gets redirected to actually solving problems together.

Speaking Their Language: From Construction-Speak to Patient Outcomes

Your client thinks in terms of patient care, community health, and staff well-being. One of the fastest ways to build trust is proving you understand their mission by translating every construction milestone into language that matters to them.

Here's how this plays out in practice during something as technical as an electrical shutdown:

Don't say: "For this shutdown, we're going to be turning off panels X, Y, and Z."

Say this: "For this shutdown, it's going to impact the power in the emergency outlets in patient rooms 1 through 8. This helps you understand which patients will be affected and what equipment you have plugged into those outlets. Because we're only turning off emergency power, you can simply unplug equipment from emergency outlets and plug into normal power outlets during the shutdown. My electrical team will be happy to assist with this if needed."

The difference is profound. Instead of panel numbers, you're talking about patient rooms and the specific impact on their equipment. Instead of speaking only in technical jargon and leaving them to figure out how it will impact the floor, you're providing clear solutions with support, showing that not only do you understand the ramifications of the work, but you are willing to take your time to help minimize their downtime.

This shift in language constantly reinforces that you understand and share their ultimate purpose: saving lives.

Translation, however, goes both ways. There's a story in the California healthcare community—I'm not even sure if it's true or merely urban legend—about a construction worker who yelled down a hospital corridor to his employee: "Get that COW out of the way!" using the acronym, which is short for Computer on Wheels, the name for the mobile nursing workstations.

Unfortunately, there was also a larger woman in the hallway at the time who believed he was calling her a cow. She was understandably offended, and according to the story, a lawsuit was filed.

Needless to say, healthcare facilities stopped using "COW" and switched to "WOW" (Workstation on Wheels). And whether true or not, the story illustrates why meetings between hospital and construction staff require establishing an understanding of what each side expects from the other. You can't speak in acronyms and industry language in situations where your directions may be misconstrued. Both sides need patience and understanding that the other doesn't necessarily know their terminology. Using full terms, like "Request for Information" instead of "RFI," or even terms that are typically known, like "Emergency Room" instead of "ER," go a long way toward bridging any possible communication gaps.

I learned this lesson the hard way early in my career. I was presenting a schedule update to a group of hospital administrators and kept referring to "the MEP rough-in" as if everyone knew what that meant. Finally, one administrator—bless her for having the courage to ask— said, "I'm sorry, but what's MEP?"

"Mechanical, Electrical, and Plumbing." I'd been working in construction so long that I forgot this wasn't common knowledge.

From that day forward, I made it a practice to define any acronym or technical term the first time I used it in a meeting, and to watch people's faces for signs of confusion. If someone looked puzzled, I'd stop and explain, no matter how basic it seemed to me.

This isn't dumbing things down—it's respecting that your audience has expertise in healthcare that you don't have, and you have expertise in construction that they don't have. The partnership works when both sides translate their specialized knowledge into language the other can understand and use.

Protecting the Patient, Not Just the Project

Healthcare construction demands a fundamental shift in priorities. It's usually the case that whatever is good for a construction project is bad for the hospital, and vice versa. It's paramount to remember that patients always come first.

This isn't just philosophy—it's practical reality that shapes every decision you make.

I was working on a large lab project—this was after I'd transitioned from consultant to Director of Construction—which required hundreds of seismic anchors to be drilled into the ceiling. The lab was located directly underneath the OR (operating rooms) where doctors conducting literal brain surgeries required absolute silence and stillness.

Even when working within approved hours, we'd get urgent calls to stop drilling if there was an emergency case or a surgery was taking longer than anticipated. This coordination made the process take significantly longer and cost more money, but it was a fact we had to accept to keep surgeons focused and patients safe.

This principle extends to every aspect of healthcare construction. You always have to know who is above, below, and on each side of your work area. You need to understand their functions and determine if vibrations, noise, or disruption will affect patient care. Then you literally build the construction schedule according to the hours when they can tolerate your activities.

I can't count how many projects have run entirely on night shifts because we simply couldn't create noise, vibration, or disruption during business hours.

On another project, we were replacing decaying infrastructure in a building that housed some of the hospital's sickest patients—an aging sewage system that finally failed. When pipes burst and raw sewage leaked onto the floor, we had to evacuate the entire department and deliver devastating news: they wouldn't be able to return for several *months*.

This wasn't even part of our original project scope—it was an emergency response to failing hospital infrastructure. But we stopped our other work, abandoned our schedules and commitments, and put the hospital's needs first. We developed a plan for minimal disruption to replace the broken pipes and all the aging infrastructure that posed future risks.

All that work had to be done at night. Pipe replacement required water shutoffs, disabling sinks and toilets throughout affected areas. We provided potable water and temporary toilets in every patient room, worked in very small phases, and maintained 6-7 hour night shifts while patients slept. Every morning by 6 AM, hospital leadership received a full report of progress and any issues.

When the department finally reopened with completely replaced infrastructure, the staff moved back into a cleaner, remodeled space.

The hospital leadership saw that we were willing to set aside project ambitions to solve their problem, and that spoke volumes about our partnership.

This is what "patients always come first" actually means. It's not a slogan—it's a decision-making framework that costs you time and money, but builds something far more valuable: trust that you genuinely care about their mission.

Spending Their Money Like It's Yours

Financial stewardship isn't just about staying on budget—it's about approaching every financial decision as if the money were coming from your own pocket.

Throughout my career, whether working as an owner's representative or managing projects for contractors, I've developed a systematic approach to cost scrutiny. When changes come in, I study the plans, study the changes, and ask the same questions every time:

> "Why can't we build this per the plans?"

> "What changed?"

> "Who caused it?"

> "Why is this the owner's responsibility?"

Sometimes costs are legitimately the owner's responsibility or beyond the contractor's control. But when contractors don't raise issues in a timely manner—when the owner could have addressed them differently—I protect the client from those cost expenditures.

I've watched contractors destroy their trust accounts through pure greed. There was one outfit that consistently bid on my RFPs when I was working as an owner's rep—a company owned by a guy who was smart as a fox but had no moral compass, specializing in bidding on projects with incomplete document sets. He was the best change-order artist I ever met, underbidding every other contractor by significant margins, then change-ordering projects to death, raising the overall cost to far more than the other contractors had bid, due to missing plan information.

The first time it happened, I chalked it up to experience. Shame on him.

The second time it happened on another project, I realized I was dealing with a predator. Shame on me for not learning the lesson.

There wasn't a third time.

That contractor lost trust permanently—and not just my trust. To this day, fifteen years later, he does not work on any projects at that hospital system. He was blacklisted. His short-term thinking—maximizing profit on a couple of projects—cost him millions in future work.

The ledger of trust is unforgiving. You can spend years making deposits, but make enough withdrawals driven by greed or carelessness, and you'll find yourself bankrupt in the only currency that really matters.

Here's the discipline I've developed over the years: Before I approve any change order—whether I'm representing the owner or managing the project for a contractor—I ask myself, "If this were my personal money, would I pay for this?" If the answer is no, I dig deeper until I understand why the cost is legitimate or find a way to reduce it.

This philosophy has, at times, put me at odds with my employers when I was working for contractors. I've had sales and executive teams push back when I've reduced change order pricing because "the client will pay it." My response has always been the same: "Maybe they will, but they shouldn't have to, and I'm not going to destroy our reputation for one project's margin."

That stance has created friction with short-term thinkers. But it's also why, when I later worked as an independent consultant, hospitals sought me out specifically. They knew I'd protect their interests even when it wasn't convenient, or financially beneficial, for me.

That's what spending their money like it's yours actually means; making the same prudent decisions with their budget that you'd make with your own. It means sacrificing short-term gain for long-term partnership and understanding that trust is worth more than any single project's profit margin.

Leading the Tough Conversations

Problems on major projects are an absolute certainty. Trust is forged in how you handle these moments. The key is bringing problems to clients early, armed with clear problem statements and potential solutions, not excuses.

There is a fine line, however. You don't want to bring every "dead fish" problem to their desk. You need experience and instincts to distinguish between issues you should handle yourself versus problems requiring their decision-making involvement. The criteria is simple: bring them the big problems, especially those that could significantly impact the schedule and cost.

It's important to stay on top of daily progress because awareness is your greatest asset. The longer you wait, the fewer resolution options they'll have. Leadership often has solutions you're not aware of. Early disclosure provides more options for positive resolutions and shows them you are managing proactively rather than reactively. I never want to hear, "if only I had heard about this sooner" from a client. When I hear that, I know I've failed.

I learned this during one of the most complex coordination challenges I've faced. I was simultaneously managing two projects sharing some of the same footprint. The pneumatic tube upgrade project had been put on hold due to permitting and budget issues. The collaborative space project—a large space with cubicles, conference rooms, and storage—was moving forward on schedule.

The problem: one crucial P-tube station was located directly in the middle of the collaborative project footprint. We couldn't demolish that space or build the planned corridor until the P-tube project resumed.

I had to deliver bad news to the project stakeholders: their project would be impacted by a completely separate project managed by different departments, leadership, stakeholders, and budgets. This was poor coordination that happened before my involvement, but, as Director of Construction, I was now responsible for the solution.

I presented two options:

Option 1: Absorb months of delay waiting for the P-tube project to restart.

Option 2: The collaborative space project absorbs approximately $1 million to relocate the P-tube station.

This was a complicated situation, as the existing station was crucial to hospital operations, handling 24/7 lab deliveries. Relocation meant building a new station outside project boundaries, getting it operational, then demolishing the old one.

They chose Option 2. Instead of a protracted work stoppage, waiting for the P-tube project to restart, we managed a delay of just two months with the $1 million cost absorption.

The stakeholders weren't happy about the lack of coordination, but because I presented the problem with clear options and realistic consequences, and because we delivered the collaborative project on time despite the major hiccup, we earned significant trust and appreciation from leadership.

Before presenting any problem, I prepare by understanding the issue, identifying root causes when possible, and bringing in anyone with relevant information. Most importantly, I develop at least one viable solution, preferably multiple options showing impacts on staff, patients, schedule, and cost.

Always give clients choices with clear consequences, rather than dumping problems on them and expecting them to figure out solutions on their own.

Here's what this looks like in practice:

Bad approach: "We've got a problem. The mechanical system doesn't fit in the ceiling space. We're going to be delayed."

Good approach: "We've discovered a coordination issue between the mechanical system and the structural beams. I've worked with our MEP engineer and identified three options: Option 1 is to redesign the duct routing, which adds two weeks and $50k but maintains all functionality. Option 2 is to lower the ceiling in this area by 6 inches, which adds one week and $30k but may impact the aesthetic you wanted. Option 3 is to use a different air handler model, which maintains schedule but adds $75k and reduces efficiency slightly. Based on your priorities, I'd recommend Option 1, but wanted you to see all the options and understand the tradeoffs."

Do you see the difference? The second approach shows you've already done the work to understand the problem and taken the time to develop viable solutions before they even ask. You're not telling them to solve your problem—you're asking them to make an informed decision about tradeoffs.

When Construction Meets Medicine: The Art of Risk Communication

Large-scale hospital shutdowns exemplify why transparency builds credibility. These operations can overwhelm medical staff if presented as a technical info dump. Instead, I learned to lead with acknowledgment of the trust being placed in me and the risks to their patients and professional reputation.

Shutdowns involve enormous complexity: circuit investigation and tracing, sequencing protocols, equipment that can't simply be turned off and on, cooling requirements, medication access systems, timing criticalities and a host of other issues that can stow or completely stop progress. If you focus on technical complexities when talking to medical staff, they won't listen. They're thinking, "What's so important that you're willing to risk my patients and staff?"

It's important to think about this from the hospital's perspective. If construction affects a patient's hospital experience, the patient doesn't blame the contractor—they blame the hospital. This damages the hospital's reputation even though it isn't the caregiver's fault.

I learned to reframe these conversations by starting with empathy rather than technical requirements. I acknowledge the weight of responsibility the medical staff is sharing with me, including both concerns about patient safety and their professional credibility, and I assure them that comprehensive planning will address these risks before any work begins.

Here's what that conversation actually sounds like:

> "Before we talk about the technical details of this shutdown, I want to acknowledge something important: You're trusting us with your patients' safety and your department's reputation. If something goes wrong during this work, your patients and their families will hold you responsible, not us. I take that responsibility seriously, and I want you to understand how we're planning to protect what matters most to you.

> "Now, let me walk you through what we're proposing to do, why it's necessary, what could go wrong, and what we're doing to prevent every scenario we can think of. And then I need you to tell me what we're missing and what concerns you have that we haven't addressed. What do you know about your operation that we don't?"

This approach is all about setting and meeting expectations, transforming the dynamic from construction imposing requirements on the medical staff, to construction partnering with staff to protect what matters most to them.

When you are upfront and transparent about potential risks you foresee, medical staff and administrators are more likely to share risks they know about that you might have missed. Together, you develop comprehensive mitigation plans.

The more experience you gain with shutdowns, the better you become at anticipating and communicating risks before they become problems. This transparency builds credibility because it shows you understand the complexity of the situation and take their concerns seriously.

I've conducted dozens of major shutdowns throughout my career, in various roles and at different hospitals, and the pattern is always the same: the projects that go smoothly are the ones where we spent the most time upfront having honest conversations about risks and building comprehensive plans with input from the people who actually work in those spaces.

The Trust Meter: Reading the Relationship

How do you actually measure trust in relationships? Typically, trust is a gut feeling, but there are specific behaviors to watch for.

The most reliable indicator is the magnitude of autonomy they give you. Trust exists on a spectrum:

Low Trust Indicators:

- The client expects notifications before every decision.
- The client wants constant contact and reports.
- The client doesn't want you speaking with contractors or architects about important decisions without them.

High Trust Indicators:

- They want you to handle everything independently.
- They only involve themselves when absolutely necessary.
- They give you full confidence to make decisions

Here's a practical way to evaluate where you stand with any client:

Autonomy Level Assessment:

1. How many decisions can you make without their approval?
2. What's the dollar threshold for changes you can authorize?

3. How often do they ask for updates versus you providing them proactively?

4. Do they introduce you to others as "our project manager" or "our partner"?

Communication Pattern Analysis:

- **High Trust:** They call when they have questions, not to check on your work.

- **Medium Trust:** Regular scheduled updates with some independent decision-making.

- **Low Trust:** Daily check-ins and approval requests for routine decisions.

Crisis Response Evaluation:

- **Strong Trust:** They call you first when problems arise.

- **Moderate Trust:** They include you in problem-solving discussions.

- **Weak Trust:** They discuss problems internally before involving you.

Early warning signs that trust is eroding mirror these low-trust behaviors. If you've made a mistake and now they want more feedback and involvement in decisions you previously handled independently, trust has clearly taken a hit. You have to accept this with understanding and work to build it back over time.

Throughout my career, I've experienced both sides of this spectrum. Early on, when I was proving myself, I operated under close supervision. As I built track records and relationships, I gained more autonomy. But I've also experienced trust erosion after mistakes, and had to patiently rebuild it through consistent performance.

The key insight is that trust levels fluctuate based on two interconnected factors: your performance and their confidence. Your goal is to consistently build toward the high-trust end of the spectrum, where you have the autonomy to do your best work without constant oversight.

Progressive warning signs include them pulling projects away or stopping new project awards entirely. When trust has "really gone off the rails," it requires a crucial conversation to see if the relationship can be repaired.

The Trust Rebuilding Process

When trust is damaged, systematic rebuilding is essential. I learned this process during the crisis I mentioned earlier—and we'll explore it in much greater detail in Chapter 6—but the framework applies to any situation where you've made a significant withdrawal from the trust account.

Phase 1 - Immediate Response (Hours):

- Stop all related work immediately if it's a safety issue.
- Take full responsibility without excuses.
- Begin thorough investigation.
- Communicate what you're doing to address the situation.

Phase 2 - Investigation and Analysis (Days/Weeks):

- Conduct root cause analysis.
- Document everything transparently.
- Listen to all concerned parties without defensiveness.
- Develop comprehensive corrective actions.

Phase 3 - Implementation and Proof (Months):

- Implement new policies and procedures.

- Demonstrate changes through consistent action.

- Provide regular updates on improvement efforts.

- Accept increased oversight during the rebuilding period.

Phase 4 - Validation and Moving Forward:

- Show measurable results from improvements.

- Gradually earn back autonomy through consistent performance.

- Use lessons learned to prevent similar issues.

The key is to remember that trust can be rebuilt, even stronger than before, but only through systematic effort and genuine change, not just apologies.

I've experienced this process from multiple angles throughout my career. Early on, I made mistakes that damaged trust and had to work hard to rebuild it. Later, as I moved into leadership roles, I had to guide others through the rebuilding process. I've also been on the client side, deciding whether to give someone the chance to rebuild that trust or to move on.

What I've learned is that people are often willing to give you a second chance if you:

1. Take full responsibility immediately.

2. Demonstrate genuine understanding of the impact.

3. Implement real changes, not just cosmetic ones.

4. Prove through consistent action that you've learned.

5. Accept that rebuilding takes time and don't rush it.

People are inherently forgiving, particularly when you own up to your mistakes and show a plan for how to rectify or minimize the impact on them. That said, people are rarely willing to give you a third chance to make the same mistake. That predatory contractor who change-ordered projects to death? He burned through his second chance on project two. There was no third opportunity.

From Crisis to Stronger Partnership

What I learned through years of building trust in various roles across different organizations is you don't build crisis management skills during a crisis. These skills must be built beforehand, through all the small, daily disciplines, trust deposits, transparent communication, and consistent follow-through on promises. The first thing to learn about crisis management is how to avoid a crisis.

When I got that text from Matt asking to talk, and when Tim suggested I take over for him, it wasn't because I'd never made mistakes. It was because when I made mistakes, I handled them with transparency and ultimately took responsibility. It was because I had made thousands of small deposits in the trust ledger; I kept promises, spent their money carefully, brought problems to them early and always with possible solutions, translated construction-speak into how something will impact the patients, and did everything in my power to protect patients over project convenience.

You are never done building trust. That initial conversation with Matt was the beginning of a new level of responsibility, where the stakes got even higher and the trust requirements became even more demanding.

Throughout my career, I've worked for contractors, hospitals, and myself. I've been the young PE trying to prove myself, the experienced PM managing complex projects, the consultant brought in to fix struggling programs, and the director responsible for entire construction portfolios. The role changes, the organization changes, but the principles of trust remain constant.

Keep your promises, even the small ones. Spend their money like it's yours. Bring up problems early, and offer solutions. Take responsibility without making excuses. Protect what matters most to them. Build systems that work without heroics.

Do these things consistently, regardless of your role or who's signing your paycheck, and you build a reputation for being someone people can trust when everything is on the line.

That doesn't just build trust, it builds the very foundation of a career built on significance rather than just success.

Your Next Steps

Start tracking your own trust transactions this week. Keep a simple log of promises made and promises kept. Note when you're asked for more involvement versus given more autonomy. Pay attention to the language you use in meetings—are you speaking to their mission or your convenience?

Most importantly, look for one opportunity to prioritize their needs over your project efficiency. It might cost you time or money in the short term, but it's an investment in the only currency that creates lasting partnerships.

Trust isn't built overnight, but it can be damaged in an instant. The good news is that when you focus on consistent deposits through small acts of reliability, transparency, and mission alignment, you build an account that can weather any storm.

Even one where a conduit drops from the ceiling.

CHAPTER 3

GROWING YOUR TEAM

Long before I ever managed a construction crew, I learned the most important lesson about teamwork…in the middle of a desert.

I was twenty, completely wet behind the ears, and trying to decide between two very different life paths. Would I follow my father's footsteps into engineering and construction, or become an experiential outdoor educator? To help figure it out, I enrolled in a leadership semester with Outward Bound—an experiential outfit that taught people how to be guides and teachers in the wilderness.

The course included twenty days in the backcountry of Joshua Tree National Park in Southern California. If you've never seen this place, imagine a vast desert with rolling topography, incredible wildlife, and mountains of rock formations that look like ancient monuments reaching toward the sky. It's spectacular and unforgiving in equal measure.

Our group had eight students, all in our early twenties, plus two instructors to teach us wilderness skills and—though we didn't realize it at the time—how to function as a team. The final test would be to get from Point A to Point B completely on our own, with an overnight stop. Twenty-two miles across the desert, navigating by compass and map, taking care of each other, making camp, and proving we'd learned what they'd been teaching us.

No problem. At least that's the sentiment we each projected on the surface. Inside, I'm pretty sure we were all extremely nervous about getting lost in the desert within the first six hours.

We hadn't realized that for the first few days in that park, we were being taught exactly how to be an effective team—and most of us were failing miserably.

There were a few "rockstars" in our group, if you'll pardon the pun. I was definitely one of them. I'd get annoyed when we had to stop for someone to even tie their shoe or take an extra breather. Frustrated, I would ask myself, "Why should I have to sit and wait for someone who didn't properly train for this trip?" I was focused on my performance, my timeline, and my idea of what excellence looked like.

Our leaders—and I have to say they really knew what they were doing—had a plan for putting rockstars like me in our place.

Instead of letting me complain about others slowing us down, they taught me to make the hike easier for members of the group who were struggling. Instead of celebrating individual achievements, they showed us how to get through necessary tasks more quickly when we worked together rather than independently.

Most importantly, they taught us to appreciate each other's strengths and weaknesses, and how to fill in any individual gaps of weakness so that all that was left was collective strength.

It took us a good three or four days of struggles and arguments before we understood these concepts and found our groove, but once we did, things started to change for the better..

When the time came for our two-day test navigating those twenty-two miles on our own, the group was ready.

My weakness was navigating with a map. (I still can't get that right, and my wife will certainly attest to that. Thank God for Apple CarPlay.) My strength was physical endurance and brute force.

In Joshua Tree, there's no water to refill your bottles, so you have to carry all your water through the desert. Ten pounds of water per person, minimum. That much extra weight slowed down people who weren't as physically strong, which hurt the whole group's progress.

I happily lightened the load of our best navigator, carrying some of their water so they could get out ahead of the group to study the terrain and topography and scope out exactly where we were headed, so by the time the group caught up, they could tell us where to go next.

We had a few people who were great at making camp food, so they focused on that in the evenings while others helped set up tents and organize gear. Everyone had a role that played to their strengths, while covering someone else's weakness.

We all had a profound sense of pride that we were doing so well working together as a team, especially because we were doing it on our own. Our leaders stepped back, trusted that we knew what we were doing, and gave us the tools to succeed.

We passed that test with flying colors.

Navigating that desert, I learned the difference between a group of individuals trying to prove themselves and a crew of people committed to making each other successful. It's a lesson that has shaped every team I have ever built.

The rockstar version of me would have sprinted ahead with the map, gotten everyone lost, and blamed others for not keeping up. The team-focused version carried extra water, supported the navigator, and helped create conditions where everyone could contribute their best.

Twenty years later, in hospitals and construction sites across the country, I'd see the same dynamic play out over and over again. Projects succeed when you have the right people in the right roles, supporting each other's strengths and covering each other's weaknesses. Things will always fail if you have a bunch of individuals more focused on their own performance than the team's mission.

That lesson would prove more valuable than any technical skill I'd ever learn.

When Rockstars Destroy Teams

Years later, I witnessed the opposite approach—and saw firsthand how destructive it could be.

I was a Director of Construction at one of California's most prestigious academic medical centers, but I wasn't the *only* director. In total, there were four of us, each managing our own hospitals and programs. One of them was our notorious rockstar. Let's call him Mack.

Mack's ego was the size of Texas. He was the longtime director with seniority, and everyone knew it. He'd been a director back when I was still in high school. This wouldn't have bothered me much—he had his hospital and program, I had mine, and my responsibility was actually about ten times the size of his—but the incoming vice president instituted new policies requiring all directors to collaborate with each other. She had good intentions, trying to form a cohesive team among the leadership group. The problem was a director's job is to direct, not take orders from other directors. We were all equals, but Mack definitely didn't see it that way.

He began meddling with my teams and my projects, instead of focusing on his own responsibilities. He was more interested in proving he was the senior guy who should have influence over everyone else's work.

I saw the writing on the wall very early. A horse built by a committee ends up looking like a giraffe. The same goes for a hospital.

I resigned on my own terms. Shortly after I left, Mack was promoted to Executive Director—exactly what his ego had been driving toward all along.

A little over a year after that promotion, Mack was fired, along with the VP who had promoted him.

The rockstar approach had finally caught up with him. Instead of building teams that could succeed without him, he had built a system that revolved around his need to ensure everyone knew he was in charge. When that system was tested, it collapsed.

They're still trying to recover from the damage.

In the Joshua Tree desert, I learned that the strongest teams are built when everyone focuses on making others successful. In that office, I watched what happens when someone focuses on being the star, even if that comes at the expense of the team..

The choice between these two approaches isn't just philosophical—it has real consequences for projects, teams, and the people whose lives depend on what we build.

The Sacred Space: Creating Your Internal Huddle

Trust with a client is impossible if you don't first have trust with your own people. The "Internal Huddle" is where you practice the brutal honesty and unwavering support that clients will eventually see.

I learned this lesson when I was working as a senior project manager for a large general contractor in the Bay Area. We were managing a medium-sized healthcare project that was starting to fall behind schedule. And the fault was ours—not the architect's, not the owner's, but ours.

That's when one of our executives paid the project a visit and asked, "Are you guys utilizing a team huddle to make sure you're prioritizing the things that have to get done and assigning champions to each task?"

To most of us on that team, it was a new concept, but I liked the sound of it and was eager to learn.

Huddles work especially well for general contractors on large construction projects: you've got a lot of different roles—executives, directors, senior superintendents, project managers, engineers, field crews. There's a lot of work happening simultaneously by a lot of different people. It's easy to get distracted or have things get fouled up because everyone's moving so fast that communication gets put on the back burner.

That executive gave us the concept and the tools to quickly implement this strategy. We all had company phones, so he showed us an app we could download to organize everything.

As the senior project manager, I entered the key information for everyone on the team. Then we went down the list of all the tasks that had to be done that day, that week, and that month. We assigned every task to a "champion"—a person best suited to succeed at that task—

plus anyone who would be supporting them. As soon as someone completed a task, they could check it off and the rest of the team would be notified immediately.

Every morning, we'd run through the completed items from the day before and all the items assigned to be finished that day, plus anything that needed to be started that day in order to finish the following day.

We did this for several months, day in and day out. And by God, that project got back on track.

The organization of the team huddle helped us effectively communicate through a lot of complex, intertwined work and helped our team straighten it out.

Admittedly, the huddle isn't the solution to everything. We already had a good team, and we each knew our role, but what the huddle gave us was visibility and accountability that we'd been missing. It created a space where problems couldn't hide and where everyone knew exactly what everyone else was working on.

The Anatomy of an Effective Huddle

Looking back, I can see why that simple system worked so well. Here's what made it effective:

Daily Consistency: Same time, same place, same format. No exceptions. When you make it routine, people plan their work around it instead of seeing it as an interruption.

We met every morning at 7:00 AM sharp. Not 7:05, not "whenever everyone shows up"—7:00 AM. If you were late, the meeting started without you and you had to catch up. That discipline sent a message: this matters enough to be on time for.

Champion System: Every task had one person accountable for completion. Shared responsibility sometimes becomes nobody's responsibility.

This was crucial. Before we began using the huddle, we'd have tasks that were sort of everyone's responsibility, which meant they were really nobody's responsibility. "Someone needs to follow up with the mechanical engineer about that duct routing." Who is someone? When the huddle started, every task had a name attached. "Mike is following up with the mechanical engineer about duct routing by end of day Wednesday."

Visible Progress: Real-time updates that everyone could see. When someone checked off a completed task, the whole team knew immediately.

The app made this transparent in a way that emails and spreadsheets never could. You could open your phone during lunch and see exactly what had been completed that morning and what was still in progress. No one could hide behind "I'm working on it" when the rest of the team could see that task had been sitting unchecked for three days.

Forward and Backward Looking: We reviewed alerts on what got done and could see what needed to happen next. This caught problems before they became crises.

The first five minutes of the meeting focused on "What got completed yesterday?" This was celebration time. We'd acknowledge the wins, no matter how small.

"Submittal package for casework went out."

"Structural inspection passed."

"Coordination meeting with facilities confirmed schedule."

These small victories built momentum.

The next ten minutes focused on "What needs to happen today and tomorrow?" This was coordination time, when we would identify dependencies, potential conflicts, and who needed support. "I can't start the ceiling grid until electrical finishes their rough-in, so I need to know by noon if that's happening today., " or "I need someone to review this RFI draft before I send it out."

Support Identification: When an assignment was given to a "champion," we also identified who would support them on each task. This prevented people from getting stuck and not asking for help. It also allowed those in support roles to know specifically what they had to do, rather than waiting around until the lead asked for help."Mike is champion for the mechanical coordination meeting, with John supporting by pulling the latest drawings and Sarah supporting by coordinating the schedule."

First, this system distributed the workload so one person wasn't drowning while others had capacity. Second, it normalized asking for help. You weren't weak for needing support—it was built into the system.

Most importantly, it created a space where you had to be honest about your progress. There was nowhere to hide, but there was also immediate support if you were struggling.

When Honesty Becomes Habit

The real power of a good huddle isn't the app or the task tracking—it's the culture it creates. When you meet every day and have to report honestly on your progress, something interesting happens. People start bringing up problems before they become emergencies.

I remember one morning when a project manager said he was worried about getting the main service connection completed on time because the utility company was giving him the runaround on scheduling. In a typical project meeting, he might have waited until the last minute to raise this issue, hoping he could solve it himself.

But in the huddle environment, he felt safe bringing it up early. That gave our Senior project manager time to make some calls, escalate the issue, and get it resolved before it impacted the schedule.

Project Manager: "I'm concerned about the utility connection. I've called them three times this week and can't get a straight answer on when they can schedule the hookup. If we don't get it done by Friday, we're going to miss our MEP substantial completion milestone."

Sr. Project Manager: "Okay, who's your contact there?"

Project Manager: "Guy named Robert in scheduling, but he keeps saying he'll call back and doesn't."

Sr. Project Manager: "I've got a relationship with their regional manager from another project. Let me make a call this morning. Mike, can you support by pulling together all our documentation showing we've met our requirements and are ready for hookup?"

Me: "Yeah, I'll have that to you by noon."

Sr. Project Manager: "Great. Let's touch base at 2 PM and see where we are. If we can't get movement by tomorrow, I'll escalate to the hospital's facilities director—they have leverage with the utility company we don't have."

Problem identified. Support assigned. Follow-up scheduled. All in about two minutes.

Without the huddle, that young project manager would have kept making calls, getting more frustrated, and maybe mentioned it to his superintendent who might have eventually escalated it. By then, we'd be up against the deadline with no good options.

The Rules of Sacred Space

For a huddle to work, it has to feel safe. There are ground rules we established—some explicit, some implicit—that made our huddle effective.

No Blame, Only Solutions: When someone admits they're behind or struggling, the first response is always "What do you need?" never "Why didn't you tell us sooner?"

I learned this rule by violating it early on. One of our project engineers admitted in a huddle that he was behind on processing submittals because he'd been pulled into crisis management on another part of the project. My first instinct was frustration, asking "How long have you been behind?"

Our then Director —older, wiser—immediately redirected the conversation by saying, "Let's figure out how to help. Who can take some of those submittals off your plate?"

It was a lesson I needed to learn. From then on, every admission of struggle was met with problem-solving, not interrogation. The result? People brought up issues much earlier, when they were easier to fix.

Problems Are Opportunities: Every issue raised in a huddle is a chance to prevent a bigger problem later. Celebrate that honesty, don't punish it.

We actually started calling out people who raised issues early: "Thanks for bringing that up now while we can still do something about it."

This positive reinforcement created a culture where people competed to identify problems early, rather than hiding them.

Check Your Ego at the Door: It doesn't matter if you're the senior superintendent or the newest project engineer—everyone's voice matters equally in the huddle.

This was hardest for the veterans who were used to their experience and position commanding automatic respect. But the huddle was a flat space. When the young PE pointed out a potential conflict in the drawings that the superintendent had missed, we praised the catch rather than defend the hierarchy.

What's Said Here, Stays Here: The huddle is for the internal team to work out problems before presenting a united front to clients and stakeholders.

This rule was crucial. We could be brutally honest about our mistakes, concerns, and uncertainties because we knew it wouldn't leave the room. When we met with the owner or design team, we focused on presenting solutions, not chaos. To get to those solutions, however, we needed a space where we could work through the chaos honestly.

Focus on Today and Tomorrow: Don't relitigate what went wrong last week. Focus on what needs to happen now and what's coming next.

Early on, our huddles would devolve into post-mortems of last week's problems. "Remember when that submittal got rejected?" "Yeah, and then we had to..." Ten minutes later, we'd still be rehashing old issues.

We instituted a rule: backward-looking content was limited to completed tasks only. If you needed to discuss a failure, that happened outside the huddle in a separate lessons-learned session. The huddle was for forward momentum only.

The goal isn't to eliminate all problems—that's impossible in construction. The goal is to create a team that identifies and solves problems faster than they can compound into crises.

Beyond the App: Building Real Accountability

The app was helpful, but the real magic happened when we stopped needing to look at our phones to know what everyone was working on. After a few months of daily huddles, we'd developed an intuitive sense of how all our work connected.

The electrical work had to be done before the drywall could start. The drywall had to be finished before the flooring could begin. The equipment installations had to happen before final inspections. Everyone understood their own timeline, plus how their work affected everyone else's.

That's when accountability stops being about checking boxes and starts being about not letting your teammates down. When the electrical foreman knew that finishing his rough-in on Tuesday meant the drywall crew could start Wednesday, he had motivation beyond just meeting his own deadline.

It's the difference between a group of people assigned to the same project and a team working toward the same goal.

I saw this shift happen over about three months. Early on, people would come to the huddle focused on their own tasks. "Here's what I'm working on." By month three, people came to the huddle thinking about the whole project. "Here's what I'm working on, and here's how it affects what you're doing tomorrow."

One morning, our MEP project manager said, "I know the ceiling guys need ductwork done in Zone 3 by Wednesday, so I'm coordinating with the sub to bring in an extra two guys tomorrow to make sure we're out of there Tuesday afternoon." Nobody asked him to do that. He just understood how the pieces fit together and made it happen.

That's when you know the huddle has worked—when accountability becomes internal motivation rather than external enforcement.

The Ripple Effect

What I didn't expect was the discipline we developed in our internal huddles starting to show up in our client meetings. We were more organized, more proactive, and more honest about challenges and solutions.

When the hospital asked about the schedule, we could give them specific, detailed updates because we'd been tracking progress daily. When they raised concerns about upcoming work, we could address them immediately because we'd already been coordinating internally.

The trust we built with each other became the foundation for the trust we built with our clients. You can't fake the kind of confidence that comes from knowing your team has your back and that problems will get solved before they become emergencies.

Later in my career, when I moved into leadership roles at other organizations, the huddle concept came with me. Some teams embraced it immediately. Others resisted—it felt like more meetings, more overhead, more time away from "real work."

The teams that embraced it consistently outperformed the ones that didn't. Look, the huddle isn't magic, but it works because it creates the conditions for excellence, including visibility, accountability, support, and honest communication.

That's the real purpose of the internal huddle, allowing your team to practice the brutal honesty and unwavering support that clients will eventually see. It's where you build the muscle memory for accountability and develop the rhythm of proactive communication.

Most importantly, it's where you learn that admitting you need help isa sign of a team that cares more about success than ego.

The Art of Letting Go: When You Can't Be Everywhere

It's one thing to believe your people can do the work. Trust is knowing you can step back and let them prove it, even when the stakes are high.

I learned this lesson when I was managing several hundred million dollars worth of work simultaneously at that academic medical center. Earlier in the book, I mentioned that large shutdowns in occupied hospitals can be your greatest success or your worst failure, with not much in between. Well, when you're juggling that much work, shutdowns inevitably overlap.

One particular weekend, we had two major shutdowns scheduled—both significant, both risky, both absolutely critical to our project timelines. Large shutdowns are typically done on Saturdays or Sundays to minimize impact on hospital operations. These teams have to perform their shutdowns perfectly and within all the constraints the hospital gave them, as well as working within the constraints the other team was creating.

And with a nod to Murphy's Law, I couldn't be on site that day.

When planning a shutdown, it's crucial that whoever is managing the team on shutdown day is heavily involved in the planning. Since I wasn't going to be there to manage either team, I had to step out of the way and trust that two of my better construction managers were ready for something this complex.

They'd have to handle all the planning and communication, negotiate the mitigation measures that had to be put in place, and execute the work according to schedule on shutdown day. This wasn't their first rodeo, but it was definitely the first time they'd be completely on their own doing something of this magnitude.

I'll admit, I was worried. My instinct was to micromanage every detail, create backup plans for the backup plans, and check in every hour. But I knew that would undermine their confidence and my goal of developing leaders who could handle these situations without me.

So I stepped back. I let them take the challenge head-on and do it their way.

Everything went…perfectly.

The client was thrilled with how smoothly both shutdowns executed. More importantly, these two managers gained tremendous confidence in their abilities to take the lead on complex, high-stakes operations. They learned they could handle the pressure, coordinate with multiple teams, and deliver results without someone looking over their shoulders.

That experience taught me that your job as a leader isn't to be indispensable, it's to make yourself dispensable by developing people who can succeed without you.

The Micromanager's Trap

Not everyone will admit it, but the truth is, we micromanage because it makes us feel important and in control. Micromanagement is actually a sign of leadership failure! It means you either hired the wrong people or you're too insecure to let good people do good work.

The construction industry is full of leaders who can't let go. They're the project managers who have to approve every RFI, the superintendents who insist on being copied on every email, the directors who show up to job sites just to prove they're still relevant.

These leaders create teams of followers, not leaders. When they leave, get promoted or even go on vacation, their projects struggle because nobody else knows how to make decisions or take ownership.

I learned this lesson from watching both good and bad examples throughout my career, in various roles and at different organizations. The best leaders I worked under—whether I was a young project engineer or a senior director—gave me room to fail, learn, and grow. The worst ones treated me like an extension of themselves, rather than a person with my own judgment and capabilities.

Early in my career I was working as a project engineer and had a superintendent who insisted on reviewing every daily report I wrote. Literally line-editing every report before they went to the owner. His rationale was "quality control," but what he was really doing was controlling the narrative and making sure he got credit for everything that went right.

The result? I stopped putting much effort into those reports because I knew they'd be rewritten anyway. I stopped thinking about how to communicate effectively with the owner because that wasn't really my job; I was just a ghost writer for his reports.

Contrast that with Marcus, my superintendent on that early MRI project. He'd read my RFIs and sometimes point out something I missed, but he never rewrote them. He trusted me to learn from my mistakes and improve. The result there? I actually learned to write good RFIs because they were mine. I took ownership of the quality because I knew Marcus trusted me to get it right.

That's the pattern I tried to repeat later in my career when I was leading teams. A leader must give people the opportunity to prove themselves when it matters. That's the only way to build trust with your team, and develop a new team of leaders.

Creating Space for Growth

When you step back and let people stretch their capabilities, two things happen: they either rise to the occasion or they don't. Both outcomes give you valuable information.

When they rise to the occasion—like my two construction managers did during those shutdowns—you've just expanded your team's capabilities. You now have people who can handle that level of responsibility, which means you can take on bigger challenges and more complex projects.

When they don't rise to the occasion, you learn something important too. Maybe they need more training. Maybe they're not ready for that level of responsibility yet. Maybe they're not the right fit for your team. Better to find out during a controlled delegation than during a crisis.

The key is creating the right conditions for success. I didn't just throw my construction managers into those shutdowns unprepared. They'd been involved in planning from the beginning. They'd managed smaller shutdowns successfully. They had the experience and knowledge they needed—they just hadn't had the opportunity to lead something this complex.

Here's how I set them up for success:

Clear Authority Boundaries: I told them explicitly what decisions they could make independently and what required my approval. "You have full authority to adjust the schedule within the day, to coordinate with medical staff on minor issues, and to deploy resources as needed. If something comes up that could affect patient safety or requires budget changes over $10k, call me."

Support Without Hovering: I made myself available by phone but told them I wouldn't be checking in. "I trust you to handle this. Call me if you need me, but assume I won't be reaching out unless I hear there's a problem."

Debrief Commitment: I promised we'd do a thorough debrief afterward, regardless of outcome. "Whether everything goes perfect or everything goes wrong, we're going to sit down Monday and talk through what happened, what you learned, and what we'd do differently next time."

That last piece was important. It took the pressure off perfection. They knew we'd learn from the experience either way, so they didn't feel like failure was catastrophic.

The Shepherd and the Janitor

Some people think leadership means having all the answers and making all the decisions. They are wrong.

Real leadership is part shepherd, part janitor. You guide people toward the right goals, then clear obstacles out of their way so they can do their best work.

The shepherd part means setting clear expectations, providing the resources people need, and making sure everyone understands how their work connects to the bigger mission. It's about creating direction without dictating every step, and protecting the team from bureaucratic nonsense.

When I was planning those shutdowns with my construction managers, I played shepherd: "Here's why these shutdowns matter to the hospital. Here's what success looks like. Here are the risks we need to mitigate. Here's how this fits into our overall program goals."

The janitor part means solving the problems your team shouldn't have to worry about. When my construction managers were planning those shutdowns, my job was to handle the politics, manage the budget approvals, and deal with any issues that were above their authority level. I cleared the path so they could focus on execution.

They didn't need to worry about explaining to the VP why we needed two shutdowns on the same weekend—I handled that conversation. They didn't need to negotiate with the facilities director about access restrictions—I took care of that relationship. They could focus all their energy on planning and executing the technical work because I'd removed all the organizational obstacles.

Too many leaders want to be the hero—the person who swoops in to save the day. But the best leaders are often invisible. Their teams succeed, their projects finish on time, and their people grow into leaders themselves. The work speaks louder than the person taking credit for it.

Throughout my career, across different roles and organizations, I've tried to be that kind of leader—more interested in developing capable people than in being indispensable. When I was a project manager at that Bay Area contractor, I tried to give my project engineers room to grow. When I was Director of Construction at that academic medical center, I tried to develop construction managers who could run programs on their own.

Did I always get it right? No. Sometimes I held on too long. Sometimes I delegated too much, too soon. But the goal was always the same: build people who could succeed without me.

When Letting Go Pays Dividends

The real payoff from that weekend wasn't just two successful shutdowns. It was what happened next.

Both of those construction managers went on to handle increasingly complex projects. They became my go-to people for the most challenging work because I knew they could operate independently. When I eventually moved on to other roles, they were ready to step up and take on even greater responsibilities.

That's the multiplier effect of good delegation. When you develop people who can handle the work you used to do, you free yourself up to take on bigger challenges. When you create leaders instead of followers, your influence extends far beyond what you could accomplish by yourself.

The construction managers I trusted with those shutdowns later became some of the most capable project leaders I've ever worked with. They developed their own teams, mentored their own people, and created the same kind of trust and capability that I'd tried to build with them.

That's how you build a legacy in this business. Don't be the person who has to do everything. Be the person who develops others to do anything.

About a year after I'd left that organization, one of those construction managers called me to talk about a particularly complex coordination challenge he was facing. We spent thirty minutes on the phone as he walked through his options. The thing that struck me was that he didn't want me to *solve* his problem. He wanted to test his thinking against someone who'd been in similar situations.

At the end of the call, he said, "Thanks. I think I know what I need to do now."

"What helped?" I asked.

"Honestly? Just talking through it out loud. But also remembering what you used to say: 'Diagnose before you prescribe.' I was jumping to solutions before I really understood all the stakeholder concerns."

That's when you know you've built something that lasts—when the principles you taught keep working even after you're gone.

Character Over Credentials: Why Your Background Doesn't Disqualify You

I started this journey carrying two sheets of drywall through snow drifts in the dead of a Montana winter.

The career that followed wasn't built on impressive credentials or advanced degrees. It was built on what my father had taught me: respect for the people who do the work, attention to the details that matter, and the understanding that relationships and problem-solving ability matter more than what's on your resume.

Years later, when I was working as a consultant at the academic medical center, the vice president started applying gentle pressure for me to give up my successful consultancy and become a W-2 employee as Director of Construction.

To deflect this pressure, I responded somewhat playfully, "I can't work for you. I only have an associate's degree." The institution required a minimum bachelor's degree to be a director and highly recommended a master's degree.

The VP chuckled and said, "I can take care of that."

Having the vice president willing to make a policy change with HR to hire me was a huge endorsement. More importantly, it validated something I'd learned over two decades in this business: institutions that understand what really matters will bend their rules for the right person.

That moment confirmed what I believed since that winter day in Montana: your background doesn't disqualify you from building something significant. Your character, work ethic, and ability to solve problems while taking care of people are the credentials that actually matter.

The construction industry is full of people who took unconventional paths to get where they are. Some of the best superintendents I know started as laborers. Some of the most effective project managers never went to engineering school. What they have in common isn't their alma mater—it's their willingness to learn, their respect for the work, and their commitment to making everyone around them more successful.

Don't let anyone tell you that you're not qualified enough, educated enough, or experienced enough to build something meaningful in this industry. The people whose lives depend on what we build don't care about your degree. They care about whether you show up, whether you keep your promises, and whether you treat their mission as seriously as they do.

That's the only credential that really matters.

Job No. 1 is the Mission: When "It's for the Kids" Changes Everything

I decided to accept the offer to become Director of Construction, where I inherited quite a few projects I hadn't been involved with from the beginning. One of them was a pediatric emergency department renovation. They were looking to expand capacity and create a more family and kid-friendly healing environment.

This was important work and everyone involved in the project was excited about it. Unfortunately, due to unforeseen conditions—not the fault of the design team or contractor—the project had fallen behind schedule, as the team worked to overcome some serious challenges.

Naturally, when a high-visibility project starts to go sideways, people get defensive. With liquidated damages in the contract and mounting pressure, the contractor, design team, and hospital stakeholders all started taking protective positions. Everyone was focused on covering themselves rather than solving problems.

That's when my boss, Matt, the vice president of Planning, Design & Construction, taught me one of the most valuable lessons of my career.

Matt is the best mentor I've had in this business, and this story is one of the reasons why. He didn't call emergency meetings to assign blame or demand explanations. Instead, he did something simple but transformative.

Whenever people would get discouraged or complain about the effort needed to make the necessary corrections, Matt would remind them with one very simple statement: "It's for the kids."

And it was. It was for the kids, and that's the only thing that mattered.

That phrase became the new rallying cry for the entire project team. Not schedules. Not budgets. Not contract provisions. Kids who needed emergency medical care were getting it in a space that wasn't designed for them, and we had the opportunity to fix that.

The transformation was immediate and remarkable.

The contractor placed their best superintendent on the project in addition to the field supervision already there. The design team had architects and engineers on site every day instead of their usual once or twice monthly visits. Matt reassured everyone that as long as we maintained a unified mission, there wouldn't be financial consequences for the delays—he wanted everyone focused on what was best for the project and, therefore, best for the hospital.

Once Matt unified the team around that mission, everything changed. Instead of being defensive and thinking about protecting their companies, people started thinking creatively about how they could make the project even better. The team worked around the clock—tirelessly but happily—to bring the project across the finish line.

Although the project finished later than originally planned, the unified mission helped make up significant ground on both schedule and cost. More importantly, the director of the pediatric emergency department was thrilled with both the effort and the result.

The real lesson wasn't about that specific project, it was about the power of connecting people to something bigger than themselves.

Why Mission Matters More Than Motivation

I learned from Matt that you can't motivate people into caring about your project timeline, but you can connect them to a mission they already care about, which will drive performance in ways that bonuses or penalties never could.

Before Matt's intervention, everyone on that pediatric ER project was competent and professional. They were doing their jobs, and thinking about this project like any old job, with deadlines, budgets, and potential liability.

After Matt connected each member of the team to the mission, they were all thinking about the kids. The scared five-year-old who needed stitches, the parents trying to comfort their sick child in an adult-sized emergency room, the medical staff trying to provide world-class pediatric care in a space that wasn't designed for their smallest patients.

When people understand that their work directly impacts patient outcomes, they stop thinking about the minimum effort required to get the job done, and start believing in what's possible. They stop watching the clock and start watching for opportunities to exceed expectations.

I've seen this principle work across multiple projects and organizations throughout my career. Whether I was a project manager for a general contractor, a consultant for a hospital, or a director managing an entire program, the pattern was always the same. Teams connected to the mission outperform teams motivated only by contracts and consequences.

Making the Connection Real

It's not enough to say "we're building a hospital" and expect people to feel connected to the mission. You have to make the connection specific and personal.

Matt didn't just say "this is important work." He said "it's for the kids" and helped everyone visualize exactly who would benefit from their extra effort.

Here's how to make mission connections that actually motivate:

Be Specific About Impact: Instead of "patient care," talk about "the cancer patient who won't have to travel to another floor for treatment." Instead of "operational efficiency," describe "the nurse who can respond to patient calls thirty seconds faster."

I learned this lesson early in my career while on a hospital expansion project. We were behind schedule and the team was burned out. The project manager kept talking about "meeting our contractual obligations" and "avoiding liquidated damages."

Nobody cared.

Then a nurse from the unit we were expanding said something very impactful in a meeting one day. She told us about a patient who had died the previous week, explaining that because the unit was so overcrowded, response times were compromised.

"When you finish this project," she said, "we'll be able to save people we're losing now."

Suddenly the crew working overtime wasn't about avoiding penalties, it was about creating capacity to save lives.

That project finished ahead of schedule.

Use Present Tense: Don't talk about future benefits. Talk about current realities. "Right now, children are getting emergency care in a space designed for adults. We're changing that."

This shifts the frame from "this will be better someday" to "today, this just isn't good enough, and we're the ones who can fix it." It creates urgency that comes from empathy, not from artificial deadlines.

Connect Daily Tasks to Outcomes: Help people see how their specific work connects to patient outcomes. The electrician installing outlets needs to know the work they are doing is ensuring life-support equipment never loses power.

I make it a practice to have medical staff visit job sites and explain how the work will impact their ability to care for patients. When an ICU nurse explains to the HVAC contractor why air pressure differentials matter for immunocompromised patients, that contractor will never again see ductwork as just another mechanical installation.

Bring in End Users: When possible, have medical staff visit the job site and talk about how the work will improve their ability to care for patients. Nothing connects a team to a mission like hearing directly from the people who'll use the space.

One of the most effective mission connections I've ever witnessed happened on a renovation project at a Northern California hospital. We were expanding a neonatal intensive care unit, and the schedule was tight. The team was good but they weren't emotionally invested. It was just another job.

Sometime after work began I visited the NICU to check in with the staff to see if everything was going ok with the project. The supervising NICU nurse confided in me how important this project was.

"The rooms you're building," she said, "will mean I never have to tell a mother that her premature baby can't have the best monitoring equipment because we're out of space. That's what you're doing here."

I told the team about this conversation in our next staff meeting. It immediately hit home, connecting everyone to the mission. The project finished three weeks ahead of schedule.

When Mission Becomes Culture

The most powerful thing about Matt's approach was that it didn't just save one project—it changed how our entire team approached their work. People started using "it's for the kids" as shorthand for doing the right thing even when it was harder or more expensive.

That phrase became part of our culture because it represented something everyone could believe in. It gave people permission to care about more than just completing tasks. It encouraged them to think about the purpose behind their work.

When your team understands that they're not just working on any old construction job, they are creating crucial healing environments and life-saving facilities, they show up differently. They pay attention to details that don't appear on any drawing. They solve problems proactively instead of waiting for direction. They take ownership of outcomes rather than just completing assignments.

I've carried this lesson through every role I've held since then. Whether I was managing projects for a contractor or leading programs for hospitals, I've always looked for ways to connect teams to the human impact of their work.

Sometimes it's as simple as bringing medical staff to project kickoff meetings. Sometimes it's just consistently translating technical milestones into patient outcomes: "When we finish this remodel, the OR will be able to handle three more surgeries per day, which means three more patients getting the treatment they need."

That's the difference between a group of people working on the same project and a team working toward the same mission. Mission-driven teams deliver outcomes that matter to people whose lives depend on what we build.

Sometimes, connecting people to that mission is as simple as reminding them, "It's for the kids."

It's for the cancer patients.

It's for the heart attack victims.

It's for the mothers giving birth.

It's for any of the thousands of people whose lives will be touched by the work we do.

That's what a connection to purpose does; it motivates through a collective sense of pride, respect and responsibility, not through fear or individual financial incentives. And it's the most powerful force in construction.

Building Your Own Crew

Looking back at that desert in Joshua Tree, I realize those Outward Bound instructors taught me something that changed the way I look at leadership: Great teams aren't born, they're built. They're built through intentional decisions about who you bring on board, how you create space for honest communication, and most importantly, how you connect everyone to something bigger than themselves.

The contrast between that desert teamwork and Mack's ego-driven selfishness couldn't be clearer. One approach builds people up and creates lasting success. The other tears people down and eventually collapses under its own weight.

Building your internal team isn't about finding perfect people, it's about creating conditions where good people can do their best work together. It's about hiring for character over credentials, because the person who carries extra water for the team will always outperform the one who sprints ahead and gets everyone lost.

Building a team is about creating sacred spaces like that Bay Area huddle, where problems can't hide and people feel safe asking for help before they need it. It's about connecting your team to the mission they're serving, whether "it's for the kids" or simply reminding people that their work keeps life-support equipment running.

Most importantly, it's learning that good leadership isn't about you. A good leader knows when to let go and trust the people you've developed. A good leader develops others who can succeed without you watching over their shoulders.

That's what it means to move from managing a crew to building a team. That's the difference between first-half thinking, focused on your own performance, and second-half leadership, focused on everyone else's success.

Your Next Steps

Before you can build trust with clients, you need to practice it with your own people. Here's where to start:

This Week:

Identify one person on your team whose background doesn't match traditional expectations but who consistently delivers results. Study what makes them effective—it's probably character traits, not credentials.

Schedule a recurring team huddle. Start small: schedule a fifteen-minute huddle at the same time each day, focused on what's getting done today and what needs to happen tomorrow.

Find one opportunity to connect a team member's specific work to the bigger mission. Instead of "install that equipment," try "this equipment helps doctors save lives—let's make sure it's perfect."

This Month:

Look for one significant task you can delegate to someone ready for more responsibility. Give them the authority to make decisions, then step back and let them prove themselves.

Practice the "shepherd and janitor" approach: guide your team toward clear goals, then clear obstacles out of their way so they can do their best work.

This Quarter:

Develop your own version of "it's for the kids"; a simple phrase that reminds your team why their work matters beyond schedules and budgets.

Create systems that make accountability feel supportive, rather than punitive. When someone admits they're struggling, make sure the first response is "What do you need?" not "Why didn't you tell us sooner?"

In construction, it's impossible to eliminate every problem. The goal is to create a team that identifies and solves problems faster than they can compound into crises.

Remember: you're not just building your current project. You're building the people who will build the next one, and the one after that. Invest in that foundation, and everything else becomes possible.

Now that you've got the right team in place, it's time to extend that same collaborative spirit beyond your internal team. The strongest internal team in the world won't succeed if they can't work effectively with the architects, engineers, and contractors who help turn vision into reality.

That's where we're headed next: from building your internal team to assembling and leading your external partners.

CHAPTER 4

BUILDING EXTERNAL PARTNERSHIPS

The phone call that led to a $250 million contract started with a simple question: "Would you like to work together again?"

It was Kevin, an architect I'd worked with years earlier on some equipment replacement projects at a major Bay Area medical center. He was now leading design for a major expansion and renovation of a county hospital south of San Francisco, and he wanted me to be one of the project leaders.

That call—and the contract that followed was the payoff from years of building a partnership based on trust, aligned mission, and genuine respect for each other's work.

But I'm getting ahead of myself. Let me tell you how that partnership actually started.

When a Firm Name Tells You Everything

I first met Kevin around 2007. At the time, I was working as an independent construction management consultant, managing several programs, including a radiology modernization program at one hospital campus and radiation oncology upgrades at two different facilities.

This was a pivotal time in my career. After working for general contractors and experiencing the constant tension between serving the client's interests and protecting your company's profit margins, I'd made the deliberate choice to work independently as an owner's representative. It meant I could focus entirely on what was best for the hospital without worrying about change order revenue or protecting a contractor's interests.

One of my responsibilities was putting out requests for qualifications and proposals for design teams to handle these equipment replacement projects. One firm that kept showing up as well-suited for this work had a name that caught my attention: "The Design Partnership."

Kevin was one of the project architect-managers there, and the firm name turned out to be more than marketing. In our first few meetings, I noticed something different about how he approached the work. He asked more questions about the client's operations than about budget or timeline. He wanted to understand why we were replacing the equipment, not just where it would go.

It came across as genuine curiosity, not a sales pitch. That made an impression.

What Partnership Actually Looks Like

Kevin and I established a good relationship—and even beyond that, a friendship—because we appreciated each other and had trust. We both deeply cared about the mission, of the program and the client.

When we started working together, all we really had to do was form alignment on what the mission was. We knew we had trust established to carry out that mission. Communication, setting expectations, and achieving results were much easier to come by because we truly enjoyed working together and had mutual respect for our respective talents in healthcare construction.

Kevin and I did several projects together over the course of the next few years, and that bond and trust only grew because of our aligned approach to projects and clients.

Here's what that partnership looked like in practice:

We Started with Mission, Not Design: Our first conversations on any project were about understanding what the client was trying to accomplish and why it mattered.

I remember during one of our early projects—a radiation oncology equipment upgrade—Kevin's first question in the kickoff meeting was, "Walk me through a typical patient's journey through this department. What works well and what doesn't?" He cared more about how the department functioned than what their budget was or when the work needed to be completed.

That question led to a thirty-minute conversation with the department director about patient flow, staff coordination challenges, and the emotional experience of cancer patients navigating treatment. By the end, we'd identified issues that weren't in the original project scope but were actually just as important as the equipment replacement itself.

We Protected Each Other's Credibility: If Kevin made a commitment to the client, I made sure my team helped him keep it. If I raised a constructability concern, Kevin took it seriously rather than getting defensive.

On one project, Kevin's electrical engineer had detailed a connection that looked great on paper but was going to be nearly impossible to build in the tight existing conditions. Instead of waiting for the contractor to raise it as a change order opportunity, I called Kevin directly, telling him "We need to talk about this detail to find a better way."

We walked the site together, looked at the actual conditions, and Kevin immediately saw the problem. He had his engineer change the detail before we even went out to bid. That saved the owner money and prevented a contentious change order negotiation during construction.

We Solved Problems Together: When challenges came up—and they always do—we'd talk through solutions before presenting options to the client. We would make sure we'd thought through the implications from both design and construction perspectives first. We wanted to bring the client solutions instead of just problems. When an unforeseen condition came up that would require a design modification, Kevin and I would work through the options together first, so when we did bring it to the attention of the client, we had several solutions already in queue.

"Here's what we found, and here are three ways to address it. Here is what we recommend and why, and here are the tradeoffs of each approach."

The client appreciated that we'd done our homework before bringing them into the conversation, saving time, money and a whole lot of frustration.

We Celebrated Small Wins: Completing complex equipment installations on time, navigating tricky phasing without disrupting patient care, solving coordination challenges were victories we shared. Every detail matters, no matter how small.

Kevin and I, along with other people in his firm that shared his principles, completed multiple complex projects over the course of a few years. That design firm recommended me several times to other clients, reinforcing that we were in this together as partners committed to the same outcome.

When Partnership Becomes Currency

Fast forward several years. My career had continued to evolve—I'd worked as a consultant for various hospitals, spent time back with general contractors, and eventually landed in a senior leadership role at a major healthcare construction firm focused on building their California Healthcare portfolio.

Kevin, meanwhile, had moved up in his own career. He was now the President for one of California's most respected healthcare architecture firms, and he'd just been selected as the architect for a major expansion and renovation of a county hospital.

That's when he called me.

He told me about the project, the client, and that he'd really like for me to be involved. Over the next several months, Kevin helped me get to know the client, and together, the two of us developed trust with them through the qualification and proposal process.

In the end, I was sure my company was hired for that $250 million contract because the client believed two things:

First, Kevin and I were very aligned and trusted each other.

Second, we understood the county's mission and proved that deepening that trust was important to us.

Think about that for a moment. A $250 million contract—potentially the biggest project of my career at that point—came to me because an architect I'd worked with years earlier on much smaller projects trusted me enough to bring me into his most important client relationship.

That is what happens when you continue to bank that trust. It's the compound interest of genuine partnership.

What Made It Work

Looking back on my relationship with Kevin and his design firm, I can identify exactly what made it different from typical architect-contractor relationships:

Sincere Care: This firm genuinely cared about their projects and the people who would use the spaces he designed. You could see it in how they talked about the work, how they responded to challenges, how they treated everyone from hospital administrators to facilities staff.

During one of those early equipment replacement projects, we had an overnight delivery for the new equipment because it was the only feasible time to get it into the building. The project manager from Kevin's firm showed up for the all nighter just to show support and let those involved know they cared. That wasn't in their contract—they did it because they cared about solving the client's problem.

Mission Alignment: We both understood our roles. We were creating environments where healthcare can happen more effectively. That shared purpose made every decision easier.

When value engineering conversations came up—and they always do—every option was evaluated through the lens of mission impact. "Yes, this substitution saves $50k, but it compromises the staff workflow we spent six months optimizing. Is that worth it?" Usually the answer was no, but because we were aligned on mission, those conversations were collaborative rather than combative.

Mutual Respect: These design partners respected construction expertise and constructability concerns. I respected design intent and the careful thinking that went into his solutions. Neither of us treated the other as an obstacle to overcome.

I learned this lesson early working with good designers. On one project, one of those round walls that architects like to design was causing concern because it was going to be the signature element of the renovation, but the way it was detailed would be expensive and difficult to build.

Instead of just saying "we can't do that," I said, "Help me understand what you're trying to achieve with this wall. What's the experience you want to create?"

The architect explained the visual impact, the way it would guide people through the space, the emotional tone it would set. Once I understood the intent, I could say, "Okay, here's a different way to build this that achieves the same effect but saves time and money."

We worked through several iterations together, and the final solution was better than either of us would have developed alone. That experience established a pattern: design intent was sacred, but the means of achieving it was negotiable.

Trust as Foundation: We didn't need contracts and formal processes to force collaboration. We trusted each other to do good work, communicate honestly, and protect the client's interests.

This trust was tested on one project when a significant design error was discovered after the design was already complete. It was clearly the architect's responsibility—a misunderstanding of the intent of the small project. The design was overkill and would cost much more than I was willing to spend.

I called the Director in charge of this client and explained the problem. His response was, "We screwed up. Here's what happened, and here's how we're going to make it right." They redid the design at no cost.

That transparency allowed us to solve the problem quickly and minimize impact to the client. If he'd gotten defensive or tried to deflect responsibility, it would have become a battle that would have cost everyone more money and damaged the relationship.

Instead, his firm took responsibility, finished the design, and absorbed the cost. The client respected that response, and the project continued without the lingering resentment that usually follows major mistakes.

Long-Term Thinking: We knew early on we were building a relationship that would span years and multiple projects. That changes how you treat each interaction.

Later in our relationship, I was moving on from that prestigious northern CA academic health institution and there was some concern about maintaining a strong relationship with Kevin's design firm and that client. It wasn't my problem anymore—my time with this client was complete. But I spent time ensuring there would be continuity.

I was happy helping them, because I knew there would be future projects where I'd need that same support.

That long-term perspective meant we didn't keep score on who was helping whom. We just helped each other because that's what partners do.

The Ripple Effect

As I stated earlier, Kevin is now leading one of California's most prominent healthcare design firms as president. I've noticed that the architects and project managers there tend to work the same way he did—asking the right questions, focusing on mission, treating construction as partners rather than vendors.

I don't know if that's because he hired people like himself or taught them his approach, but it's consistent enough that you can see his influence.

I've also noticed that my relationship with Kevin opened doors to other architects at his firm. When they needed a construction partner who understood their approach, I'd get the call. That network effect has been worth far more than any single project.

What This Means for You

I've worked with dozens of architects and engineers over my career, in various roles and at different organizations. Some were technically brilliant but difficult to work with. Some had impressive portfolios but treated construction as an afterthought. Some were perfectly competent but just went through the motions.

And then there were people like Kevin—architects and engineers who understood that great buildings come from great partnerships.

The difference lies in the approach, the shared values, and a genuine commitment to the mission over ego.

When you're selecting design partners for your next project—whether you're a hospital owner, an owner's representative, or a contractor bidding work—you can look at portfolios all day long. But what you really need to understand is if they approach this work as a partnership or a transaction? Do they care about your mission, or just their fee? Will they still be taking your calls when problems arise, or will they disappear when things get difficult?

The best way to answer those questions is by watching how they've built relationships over time, how their past clients talk about working with them, and whether their firm culture reflects genuine partnership or just says the right words.

In the next sections, I'll show you exactly what to look for and how to build these kinds of partnerships yourself. Because the strongest internal team in the world will only succeed if they can work effectively with designers who share their commitment to mission and partnership.

The phone call from Kevin taught me that the best business development strategy is doing good work with good people and building relationships that compound over time.

That lesson has been worth far more than $250 million.

The Team Behind the Name

My first real lesson in vetting design teams came early in my career as an owner's rep working for a Bay Area Hospital on my first project for them. I was leading a project to take an existing medical office building, tear apart the ground floor, and build a modern MRI suite.

I'd been chosen for this assignment because of my success on that earlier MRI project with Marcus, and I was eager to prove to the radiology department that I could handle something this important.

The day of design team interviews arrived, and I walked into a conference room packed with what looked like seasoned professionals. They were all chatting comfortably with each other before the interview started. I didn't know any of them.

I came prepared with my list of questions—the kind a young, inexperienced interviewer thinks to ask. What's your MRI experience? What challenges have you faced? What does your fee structure look like? All the standard stuff.

Then Ralph, the principal of the architecture firm, surprised me.

"Mike, if I may, let me tell you a little bit about us and this team."

Ralph went through each member of his team and explained why they were valuable. He introduced every member of the engineering firms and the structural engineering firm, expressing his own personal trust and experience working with each one of them. Then he explained their mission—wanting to help this medical center grow into one of the best in the country and expand the radiology program.

His passion poured out of him. It was actually a very moving speech.

At some point during the interview, I asked what was probably a dumb question. It got a few chuckles. I asked the entire group: "How much experience do all of you have working with each other?"

It turned out these firms all shared the same types of values and had been working together—not only at this medical center, but at other facilities as well—for years. These people were a team with established relationships, proven collaboration, and shared mission.

Naturally, they sailed through the interview. My panel and I agreed this was the team we wanted to move forward with. And during that six-month project, I really got to see a high-performing design team in action. They set the bar for me in terms of the qualities I should be paying attention to.

Ralph became one of my first great mentors in the principles and values I've talked about in this book. But that first interview taught me something crucial about vetting design teams: you're hiring an architecture firm or an engineering firm, but you're also putting together a team, and the relationships within that team matter as much as individual capabilities.

What to Actually Look For

Here's what I learned from that experience, and from working with dozens of design teams since then, across various roles and organizations:

Look for Established Relationships: When firms have worked together before, they've already figured out their communication patterns, resolved their typical conflicts, and developed mutual respect.

A design team that's worked together on five previous projects will outperform a collection of individually brilliant firms that are meeting each other for the first time. The coordination, the constructability reviews, the problem-solving—all of it flows more smoothly when people already know and trust each other.

I learned this lesson the hard way on a project where the architect selected engineers they'd never worked with before—choosing them based on low fee rather than proven collaboration. The mechanical and electrical engineers couldn't agree on coordination responsibilities. The structural engineer missed meetings because he was juggling too many projects. The architect spent half their time mediating disputes between engineers instead of actually designing.

We finished that project, but it was painful. Since then, I've always asked, "How long have you worked together as a team? What projects have you completed together? What did you learn about working together that will make this project better?"

Watch How They Talk About Each Other: Ralph didn't just list credentials. He talked about his trust in the engineers, his experience with them, and why he valued their contributions. That told me more than any portfolio could.

If the architect dismisses or minimizes the engineers during the interview, that's a red flag. If they can't name specific people who'll be working on your project, that's a problem. If they talk about other firms as vendors rather than partners, you're seeing a preview of how your project will run.

Pay attention to body language too. Do they make eye contact with each other when discussing the project? Do they build on each other's points or talk over each other? Do they laugh together or maintain professional distance?

The best design teams I've worked with have an easy camaraderie that you can't fake. They genuinely like working together, and that shows up in how they interact during interviews.

Ask About the Actual Team, Not Just the Firm: The principal who shows up to sell the work might be brilliant, but if they're not the person who'll be managing your project day-to-day, you need to meet who will be. And you need to meet the engineers as well as the architect. You need to understand who's actually doing the MEP design, the structural calculations, the civil work.

I've seen too many projects where the A-team sold the work and the C-team delivered it. Don't let impressive credentials at the firm level distract you from vetting the actual people who'll be working on your project.

On one project I managed when I was serving as an owner's representative, the architecture firm sent their senior principal and their most impressive portfolio to the interview. We were sold. Then the project started and we discovered that principal would visit the site maybe once a month. The actual project manager was a junior architect with minimal healthcare experience who was quickly overwhelmed by the complexity.

By the time we realized the bait-and-switch, we were too far into the project to change lanes. We made it work, but it was a struggle. Now I insist on meeting the actual project team during interviews, and I put their names in the contract: "The following individuals will be assigned to this project and may not be changed without owner approval."

Listen for Mission Connection: Ralph didn't lead with technical capabilities. He led with the team's mission; helping this medical center become one of the best in the country. That told me his team understood they were contributing to something larger than a regular job.

Firms that lead with mission tend to make better decisions throughout a project. When tough trade-offs come up—and they always do— teams focused on mission will prioritize what actually matters instead of what's easiest or most profitable.

I've noticed a pattern: designers who talk primarily about their awards and their impressive portfolio are usually focused on using your project to enhance their reputation. Designers who talk about understanding your mission and solving your problems are usually focused on your success. Choose accordingly.

Trust Your Gut on Chemistry: That conference room full of people chatting comfortably before the interview started? That wasn't random. These people genuinely enjoyed working together. You could feel it in how they interacted, communicated, and supported each other's points during the interview.

Chemistry matters. Anybody can fake the "we're a great team" performance some firms put on, but it's imperative to hire a team with genuine respect and camaraderie. When problems arise—and they will—you want a team that already knows how to work through conflict without it becoming personal.

I once interviewed a design team that gave technically perfect answers to every question. Their portfolio was impeccable. Their credentials were outstanding. But something felt off—they were almost too polished, too scripted. There was no warmth, no evidence they actually enjoyed working together.

We went with a different team that had a less impressive portfolio but obvious chemistry. That decision paid off when we hit a major unforeseen condition mid-project. The team's ability to work together under pressure, brainstorm solutions collaboratively, and support each other through the stress made all the difference.

The Questions That Actually Matter

After that first Bay Area interview with Ralph's team, I started asking different questions in design team interviews, regardless of which role I was in—contractor, consultant, or owner's rep.

"How long have you worked together as a team?" If they're cobbling together firms for this specific proposal, that's not necessarily disqualifying, but you need to know. If they've been working together for years, that's valuable and should factor into your decision.

"Tell me about a project where you had to solve a major problem together." This reveals how they handle conflict, who takes leadership in crisis, and whether they actually collaborate or just coordinate.

"Who specifically will be working on this project, and can we meet them?" If the answer is vague or the firm tries to avoid committing to specific people, that's a red flag.

I want names. I want resumes. I want to meet them in the interview or immediately after. And I want those names in the contract so they can't swap them out later without my approval.

"What's your approach when construction raises a constructability concern?" The answer tells you whether they see construction as partners or obstacles. Good design teams welcome constructability input early. Bad ones get defensive.

The best answer I've heard came from an architect who said, "We assume construction knows things we don't. When they raise a concern, our first response is always 'help us understand what you're seeing.' We want to know if there's a better way to build what we're trying to achieve, or if we need to rethink what we're trying to achieve."

The worst answer came from an architect who said, "We design it correctly the first time, so we don't usually get constructability concerns." That level of arrogance is a deal-breaker. Everyone makes mistakes. Everyone misses things. The question is how you handle it when it happens.

"When things go wrong—and they will—who am I calling and what happens next?" This cuts through all the polish and gets to what really matters—accountability and responsiveness when things go sideways.

Good design teams give you direct cell numbers and commit to response times. "You'll have my cell and the project manager's cell. If you call during business hours, you'll get a response within an hour. If it's after hours and it's an emergency, you'll get a callback within 30 minutes."

Bad design teams give you vague reassurances: "We're always available to our clients." That's not an answer. That's a dodge.

When the Interview Isn't Enough

The interview can tell you a lot, but it's not everything. If possible, talk to their past clients—go beyond the references they provide to learn from people who've worked with this actual team. Ask specific questions:

- Did the people who showed up to sell the work actually do the work?

- How did they handle problems and changes?

- Would you hire this team again?

- What would you do differently if you could start over?

Visit a project they're currently working on if possible. See how they interact with the construction team, how they handle site issues, whether they're engaged or distant. You'll learn more in 30 minutes on their active job site than in hours of interviews.

I once was considering a design team for a major project when I was working as an owner's rep. Their interview was perfect. Their portfolio was stunning. But I decided to make an unannounced visit to one of their active projects.

What I found was telling: the architect hadn't been to the site in three weeks. The contractor told me getting RFI responses took two weeks minimum. The project was behind schedule and over budget, and the design team was nowhere to be found.

We didn't hire them. The interview performance didn't match the reality of how they actually worked.

Check their responsiveness during the proposal process. If they're hard to reach or slow to respond before they have your contract, they'll be worse after.

The Team That Taught Me

That Bay Area project with Ralph's team showed me what good teamwork looks like. They communicated clearly. They responded quickly to RFIs. When constructability issues came up, they worked with us to find solutions instead of defending their original design. They showed up to the site regularly for milestone meetings and to actually understand how the work was progressing.

More importantly, they made everyone around them better. The contractors respected them because they respected contractors. The hospital staff trusted them because they took time to understand operations. The project succeeded because of how well the team worked together.

That's what you're really vetting for. You want the team that will make your project—and everyone working on it—more successful.

Remember, at the end of the day, you're not buying a design. You're buying a partnership. And partnerships are only as strong as the relationships within the team.

Years later, as my career evolved through different roles and organizations, I carried those lessons with me. Whether I was selecting design teams as an owner's representative, collaborating with them as a contractor's PM, or managing them as a director overseeing programs, I always looked for the same qualities Ralph's team demonstrated: established relationships, genuine mission alignment, mutual respect, and the chemistry that can't be faked.

The designers who understood that healthcare construction is about partnership are the ones who became repeat collaborators, regardless of which organization I was working for at the time.

From Opposite Sides to the Same Team

Here's the reality most contractors won't admit out loud: we've all been burned by architects or engineers at some point. The slow RFI response that held up critical work. The change order challenge citing "design intent" when the plans clearly didn't show what they claimed. The defensive pushback when constructability concerns were raised.

It's easy for contractors to fall into an adversarial mindset: "We're the contractor, not the architect. These plans aren't complete, so the owner's going to get change orders." And when contractors take that position, design teams naturally get defensive. The relationship becomes transactional at best, combative at worst.

I've noticed that the older, more seasoned construction and design professionals have experienced both failures and successes working across this divide. They've felt the frustration of working with "the other side of the table," but they've also learned that best projects happen when there are no sides—just one team solving problems together.

Throughout my career, I've worked in roles that put me on different "sides" of this relationship. As a project manager for contractors, I've been frustrated by incomplete designs. As an owner's representative, I've watched contractors and designers point fingers at each other while the owner's money and schedule burned. As a director managing programs, I've had to mediate disputes that should never have become disputes.

What I've learned is that the "side" you're on matters far less than whether you approach the work as partnership or transaction.

What Actually Works

You can force collaboration through contract structures. CM-at-risk with GMP agreements require contractor involvement during design phases, creating real-time feedback opportunities as the design moves through schematic, design development, and construction documents. That's one way to solve the problem.

But that's not really what we're talking about here, is it? We're talking about the approach and soft skills that promote genuine collaboration, regardless of contract type.

Here's what I've learned works, from experiencing this dynamic in multiple roles:

Less Meetings, More Site Walks

The more the design team gets out to the field and looks at their design in person, the better. Walking the site with contractors and discussing what they're seeing on the plans versus what's challenging from a constructability standpoint consistently produces better results than formal review meetings.

There's something about standing in the actual space, looking at the actual conditions, that changes the conversation. The architect sees why that beam location creates a problem. The engineer understands the access constraints. The structural engineer recognizes the conflict with existing conditions. Problems that would take three rounds of RFIs and marked-up drawings to resolve get solved in a fifteen-minute walk.

I learned this lesson on a complex renovation project at a Northern California hospital when I was working as an owner's rep. We had weekly coordination meetings in the conference room—PowerPoint presentations, marked-up drawings, the whole formal process. Progress was slow and tensions were building.

One day, the mechanical contractor said in frustration, "Can we just walk this together? I need you to see what I'm seeing."

We spent 90 minutes walking the space with the architect, the engineers, and the contractor. We resolved more issues in that walk than we had in the previous month of formal meetings. From that point forward, we did site walks first, formal meetings second.

Mutual Respect Starts at the Top

The lead director or project manager needs to facilitate mutual respect between construction and design teams. If the project leadership treats designers as adversaries or obstacles, the field teams will follow that lead. If leadership treats designers as partners solving the same problems, collaboration follows naturally.

This means checking the "us versus them" language. Instead of "the architect screwed this up," try "we have a coordination issue we need to solve together." Instead of "the contractor didn't read the plans," try "we need to clarify this detail."

It sounds like small stuff, but language shapes culture. The words leadership uses signal whether this is a collaborative project or a blame-focused one.

I've been in rooms where the owner's rep would say things like "your architect made another mistake" to the hospital administration. That language immediately creates an adversarial dynamic. The architect goes into defensive mode, the contractor smells blood in the water and starts thinking about change orders, and suddenly everyone's protecting themselves instead of solving problems.

Compare that to, "We discovered a coordination issue between disciplines. The design team is working on solutions and we'll have options for you tomorrow." Same problem, completely different framing. One creates adversaries, the other creates partners.

Communication Over Documentation

I've never liked to burden teams with too many meetings, but I certainly want to encourage communication—a lot of it. Talk about schedule, materials, progress, constructability issues, value engineering opportunities, and cost concerns. Talk about everything.

The more of a roundtable the project leadership can create, the better it's going to go.

This doesn't mean adding more formal meetings to the schedule. It means creating space for informal communication. The mechanical engineer who walks the site to discuss an RFI before it even gets drafted. The architect who stops by the job trailer to review a detail that's being installed tomorrow. The structural engineer who takes a field call about a connection that looks different than the drawing.

These informal conversations prevent problems instead of just documenting them after they occur.

When I was managing large programs, I made it a point to have the architects' and engineers' phone numbers in my cell, and I'd text or call for quick questions rather than waiting for the next formal meeting. "Hey, quick question about this ceiling height—can you call me when you have five minutes?"

That kind of informal, frequent communication builds relationships and solves problems before they need formal RFIs and change orders.

Build Trust Through Small Wins

Start with easy collaborations that build confidence. When the architect provides a quick turnaround on a simple RFI, acknowledge it. When the contractor suggests a value engineering idea that improves the design, give them credit. When the engineer shows up for a site walk on short notice, recognize the effort.

These small acknowledgments build trust that makes harder conversations possible when the need arises. When you hit a real problem—and you will—you'll have a foundation of goodwill to work from.

I make it a practice to send quick thank-you emails after particularly helpful interactions:

> "Thanks for turning that submittal around in 24 hours—it kept us on schedule."

"I appreciate you taking time for the site walk yesterday. The solutions we came up with were better than what any of us would have developed alone."

Those small gestures accumulate. Six months into a project, when you need someone to go above and beyond during a crisis, they're more likely to do it if you've been acknowledging their efforts all along.

Address Problems Early and Directly

The worst contractor-designer relationships happen when problems fester. The contractor stews about slow RFI responses but doesn't say anything until it affects the schedule. The architect gets frustrated with field changes but doesn't address it until the problem compounds. The engineer feels blindsided by constructability concerns that could have been raised earlier.

Have the tough conversations early.

> "We're struggling with RFI turnaround times. Can we talk about how to streamline the process?"

> "We're seeing field changes that weren't in the submittal. How can we catch these earlier?"

> "This detail is going to be challenging to build. Can we walk through some options?"

Direct, honest communication early prevents defensive, adversarial communication later.

I learned this lesson on a project where the structural engineer was consistently missing our deadlines for drawing revisions. Instead of complaining to the owner or building a change order case, I called the engineer directly and said, "I know you're juggling multiple projects. Help me understand what's creating the bottleneck on your end."

Turns out they were understaffed and overwhelmed. Once I understood the real issue, we could solve it: the owner agreed to adjust some deadlines to give the engineer breathing room, and in exchange the engineer committed to better communication about what was realistic.

If I'd just complained instead of calling, the relationship would have deteriorated and the schedule would have suffered.

The Payoff

When contractors and designers work as genuine partners, projects run differently. RFIs get resolved faster because there's trust and open communication. Constructability issues get addressed in the design phase instead of becoming field problems. Value engineering becomes creative problem-solving instead of cost-cutting battles.

More importantly, everyone enjoys the work more. Construction is hard enough without artificial barriers created by adversarial relationships. When you trust the people you're working with, respect their expertise, and you're all focused on the same mission, the daily grind becomes something you can actually take pride in.

The best projects I've worked on—whether as a contractor's PM, an owner's rep, or a director managing programs—weren't the ones with the most impressive designs or the highest budgets. They were the ones where construction and design teams genuinely liked working together, respected each other's contributions, and solved problems as partners.

That kind of collaboration doesn't happen by accident. It happens when project leaders—whatever role they're in—deliberately create conditions for partnership instead of perpetuating the adversarial traditions of our industry.

Your Next Steps

If you're a contractor looking to build better relationships with design teams:

This Week:

Invite the design team for a site walk instead of sending another RFI email. Walk the problem together.

Acknowledge one thing the design team did well—a quick response, a helpful clarification, showing up when needed.

Check your language in team meetings. Are you talking about "we" or "us versus them"?

This Month:

Establish informal communication channels with key design team members. Make it easy to have quick conversations before problems become formal issues.

Propose one value engineering idea as an opportunity to improve the project, not as criticism of the design.

Ask the design team what would make their job easier. Then actually help with it if you can.

If You're an Owner or Owner's Representative:

Set the tone that design teams are partners, not adversaries. Make this expectation clear to your contractors from day one.

Create opportunities for informal collaboration—site walks, coordination meetings that focus on problem-solving rather than blame assignment.

Build trust through consistent, respectful communication even when problems arise. The way you handle the first conflict sets the pattern for everything that follows.

If You're a Designer:

Show up to the job site. Often. That means showing up for formal meetings, but also to see the work in progress and be available for quick questions.

Respond to constructability concerns with curiosity, not defensiveness. "Help me understand what you're seeing," is the most powerful phrase in your vocabulary.

Remember that contractors live with the consequences of your design decisions. Treat their expertise with the respect it deserves.

The strongest internal team and the best design partnerships in the world still need daily discipline to maintain excellence. That's where we're headed next—how to turn good intentions into consistent results through the power of predictable routines.

Success isn't about heroic efforts when things go wrong. It's about the small, daily disciplines that prevent most problems from happening in the first place.

CHAPTER 5

THE RHYTHM OF EXCELLENCE

Sustaining Performance Without Burning Out

The thing about walking pneumonia is that you can ignore it for a while.

It started as just a cold during the CyberKnife project at a major Bay Area medical center—the one I told you about in Chapter 1. The project where our team worked around the clock, running three shifts a day to meet that impossible four-month deadline and earn the million-dollar equipment upgrade.

I was so proud of that project. We finished two weeks early. The client was thrilled. It became one of my signature success stories, proof that dedication and hard work could accomplish anything.

What I didn't tell you in Chapter 1 was what that "success" actually cost.

I was there for most of those shifts—not all three each day, but enough that sleep became optional and rest became something other people did. That cold I was ignoring? It didn't go away. It got worse. But I kept showing up, because the project needed me, because I cared, and because that's what dedicated professionals do.

Until the day I couldn't ignore it anymore.

Walking pneumonia. The doctor gave me strict orders to rest until it passed. My body had finally overruled my ambition. But that wasn't the only cost.

That marriage I mentioned in the introduction? The one that ended in divorce? A large part of that was me making a choice—over and over again—to work rather than invest time in my family. I told myself it was temporary, that after this project things would be different, that I was building a future for us.

I was lying to myself.

I've learned the hard way that if the success of a project depends on people pushing themselves too hard, it's actually not a successful project.

Now, everything ended well with the CyberKnife project. The pneumonia healed. The client was happy. It looks great on my resume. But those were real costs—my health, my marriage—and no project deadline is worth that price.

The problem is, I didn't learn this lesson from that experience. I just kept grinding. The pneumonia was a warning shot I ignored. The divorce was a consequence I rationalized away. It took something much more serious—a ruptured appendix that turned into life-threatening sepsis in 2025, leaving me in a hospital bed for over a month—before I finally understood what I should have realized years ago.

I'd spent my career building hospitals, and I nearly died in one because I didn't know how to stop working long enough to take care of myself.

The Compound Interest of Bad Choices

In Chapter 1, I told you about the power of small, consistent actions compounding into extraordinary results. That daily routine at that Southern California hospital—the morning job walks, the persistent RFI work, the attention to detail—built trust and success over time.

What I haven't mentioned until now is that the same compound interest applies to bad choices.

Skipping one meal to finish a report doesn't seem like a big deal. Working through one cold because the project is critical won't kill you. Missing one family dinner because of a "fire" only you can put out at the job site is understandable.

But when "just this once" becomes your operating system, pushing through exhaustion becomes your identity, and proving your dedication through self-destruction becomes normal, that's when small bad choices compound into crisis.

My cold became walking pneumonia because I didn't rest when I should have. My marriage suffered because I chose work over family so many times that "just this once" became "always." The sepsis that nearly killed me in 2025 was the culmination of decades of treating my body like it was optional equipment rather than the foundation for everything else I was trying to accomplish.

The insidious thing about this pattern is how gradual it is. You don't wake up one day and decide to destroy your health and relationships. You make a series of small choices that seem reasonable in the moment—this project is too important, this deadline really matters, this client needs me—and before you know it, you've built a life that's fundamentally unsustainable.

I look back at that CyberKnife project now and I'm still proud of what the team accomplished. But I'm also clear-eyed about what it cost and whether that trade-off was worth it.

It wasn't.

Why Hustle Culture Destroys Good Contractors

I described in the Introduction how I bought into the industry's hustle culture—wearing 60-hour weeks like armor, treating burnout as a badge of honor. But what I didn't explain there was the systemic business problem this creates, and why it's destroying companies, not just individuals.

Here's what that culture actually creates: a revolving door of burned-out talent and a business model that destroys the people who do the work.

Think about how general contractors typically operate. They hire young project engineers and project managers, load them up with work that requires 60-hour weeks, and extract every ounce of productivity they can get. The overhead and general conditions costs look great on paper.

But what's the real cost?

You spend three to five years training these people—teaching them your systems, standards, and way of doing things. You invest in their education, deal with their mistakes, hold their hand while they learn the business. Just when they're finally valuable, and they've absorbed all that institutional knowledge to operate independently, they leave. They go work for your competitor.

Think about that math for a minute. All that investment in recruitment, training, and development—gone. And worse, you've just trained your competition's future leaders for free. They get fully competent professionals who already know how to manage complex projects, and you get to start over with someone new who'll make all the same mistakes while you pour another three years into training them.

The cycle perpetuates because "that's how it's always been done." But it doesn't have to be this way.

The hidden cost of hustle culture isn't just individual burnout—it's the complete failure to build institutional knowledge. When people leave after five years instead of staying for twenty, you lose all the lessons learned, relationships built, and trust you established. Every project becomes a training ground instead of leveraging deep expertise.

Meanwhile, the companies that figure out sustainable workloads get something valuable: retention. They build teams of senior people who actually remember the lessons learned from projects ten years ago. They create cultures that attract the best young talent, not just the desperate ones willing to destroy themselves for a paycheck.

I'm not saying healthcare construction is ever going to be a nine-to-five job. The work is complex, the stakes are high, and sometimes you have to put in long hours. But there's a difference between occasionally pushing hard when it matters and making unsustainable grinding your default operating system.

One builds careers and institutional knowledge. The other destroys both.

Discipline vs. Grinding Yourself Into the Ground

Here's where people get confused: they think I'm advocating for working less or caring less or accepting mediocrity. That's not what I'm saying at all.

The daily routines I described in earlier chapters—those morning job walks at that Southern California hospital, the perfect year-long reporting record, the daily team huddles—those all require discipline. Real discipline. The kind where you show up consistently even when you don't feel like it, where you do the small unglamorous work that makes projects succeed.

That's not grinding. That's sustainable excellence.

Grinding is what I did during the CyberKnife project—working three shifts' worth of hours, ignoring my health, sacrificing everything else in my life on the altar of one deadline. That's not discipline. That's self-destruction dressed up as dedication.

The difference comes down to this: discipline is about building systems that you can maintain indefinitely. Grinding is about forcing yourself to do unsustainable things until something breaks—your health, your relationships, your judgment, or the project itself.

Think about those daily job walks I did. That was discipline. Showing up at 6:30 every morning, rain or shine, and investing 30 minutes in building relationships and catching problems early. I could do that every day for years because it was sustainable. It didn't require me to sacrifice my health or my family. It just required consistency.

Now compare that to working 12-hour days for months on end. That's grinding. You might be able to maintain it for a while, but eventually something's going to break. Your body will force you to stop, like mine did with pneumonia. Your relationships will crumble from neglect, like my marriage did. Your judgment will deteriorate from exhaustion, leading to mistakes that could have been avoided.

The irony is that grinding often produces worse results than disciplined consistency. When you're exhausted, you make bad decisions. When you're stretched too thin, you miss details. When you're sacrificing everything for one project, you're not building the relationships and systems that create long-term success.

Here's how to tell if you've crossed the line from discipline to grinding:

Discipline looks like this:

- You have routines you can maintain indefinitely.
- You're building systems that work even when you're not there.
- You're making deposits in relationships, not just withdrawals.
- You can sustain your current pace for years, not just months.
- You're preventing problems, not constantly fighting fires.

Grinding looks like this:

- You're constantly telling yourself "just until this project is done."
- Systems only work when you're personally involved.
- You're making withdrawals from your health and relationships.
- You know your current pace isn't sustainable but you keep doing it anyway.
- You're always in crisis mode, always reacting, always behind.

The question isn't whether you work hard. The question is whether the way you're working can be sustained long enough to actually matter.

The Warning Signs You're Breaking

Looking back, I can see all the warning signs I ignored. The cold that wouldn't go away. The exhaustion that sleep couldn't fix. The fact that I couldn't remember the last time I'd had an unhurried conversation with my spouse.

I told myself these were just the costs of success. They were temporary sacrifices I had to make to get ahead. The problem would fix itself once I got past this deadline, or this project, or this busy season.

You know where this is going. There was always another deadline, or project, or busy season.

Here are the warning signs I wish I'd paid attention to, both personally and professionally:

Personal Warning Signs:

- Physical symptoms you're pushing through instead of addressing.

- Relationships suffering from consistent neglect.

- Using work as an excuse to avoid dealing with problems at home.

- Feeling relieved when you're at work because it's "easier" than being present for your family.

- Your identity completely wrapped up in your job title and accomplishments.

- Can't remember the last time you did something just because you enjoyed it.

Professional Warning Signs:

- Quality of work declining even though hours are increasing.

- Making mistakes you wouldn't have made when well-rested.

- Team morale dropping because they're following your unsustainable example.

- Constantly in reactive mode instead of proactive planning.

- Using "busy" as a status symbol or excuse.

- Resentment building toward people who have better work-life balance.

The Warning Sign I Missed Most: When people who cared about me expressed concern, I dismissed it. My wife pointed out that I was never home. Friends suggested I constantly looked tired. Colleagues mentioning that I seemed stretched too thin.

I heard all of it as noise. Proof that they didn't understand how important my work was or how much was riding on this project. They didn't know how dedicated I needed to be to succeed.

I didn't understand that the people who care about you often see the warning signs before you do. They're not trying to hold you back; they're trying to keep you from destroying yourself.

If you're managing a team, these warning signs apply to them too. When you see your project engineers consistently working late, your superintendents stop taking vacation days, or someone's quality of work starts declining despite putting in more hours, these are symptoms of a system that's breaking people.

Your job as a leader isn't to celebrate their dedication. It's to ask, "What do I need to do to help you fix that?"

The truth that nobody wants to admit? When you burn out, the projects will continue without you. The company will hire someone else. The work will get done. The industry that consumed you will just move on to the next person in line.

Your family can't just move on to the next person in line. . Your health won't fix itself. Your relationships won't work out unless you're there to put the work in. .

The things you sacrifice for unsustainable success don't come back.

Do You Know What Your Big Rocks Are?

The biggest change after my sepsis health scare was committing to a simple philosophy, and my life has been much more balanced ever since. This is a big part of the second-half mentality. Instead of chasing success, you make a decision to start chasing significance.

I was reminded of a lesson I'd heard before but hadn't truly internalized: the Big Rocks philosophy.

Imagine you have an empty jar. This jar represents the finite time you have in your life. Now imagine you have a pile of large rocks, some smaller pebbles, and a bucket of sand.

The Big Rocks represent your most important, life-defining priorities—the core of a significant life. For me, those are my faith, my family, and my health. These are non-negotiable. If I don't have any one of these three things, my life will be off balance, unhealthy, and just about everything else will begin to suffer.

The pebbles represent other important things that make life rich— your career, your friendships, your personal goals. These matter, but they're not the foundation.

The sand represents all the small stuff—the daily emails, the trivial tasks, the endless distractions that compete for your attention.

Here's the lesson: if you start by pouring the sand into the jar, it quickly fills the space, leaving no room for the pebbles or the Big Rocks. This is how many of us live—reacting to the urgent but unimportant, allowing the relentless grind to consume our time until there's no space left for what truly matters.

However, if you place your Big Rocks in the jar first, they form the foundation. The pebbles can then be added, easily settling into the gaps between the larger rocks. Finally, you can pour in the sand, which effortlessly fills the remaining space.

The lesson is simple but profound: if you don't intentionally schedule and protect your Big Rocks first, you will never fit them in. The sand will always expand to fill your life.

A successful career and a significant life are built not by managing the sand, but by making sure your Big Rocks always fit in your jar.

What This Actually Looks Like

For me, Sundays are nonnegotiable because my faith is important to me. Now, I know some of you are thinking, "Sometimes Sunday is the only day we can get something done in a hospital." I understand that. I'm not telling you not to work on Sundays. That's just a personal thing for me.

Maybe yours is college football on Saturdays, the weekly poker game with your life-long friends or coaching your kid's baseball team. The point is blocking time for the things that are truly important to you.

For me, that's time to spend with my family, going to church, and getting some much needed rest. That essentially satisfies my three Big Rocks every week. When Sunday comes, I'm not checking email, thinking about project schedules, or solving problems for contractors. I'm present for the things that actually matter.

The most successful people I've encountered—and sometimes been mentored by—definitely know how to keep their life in balance. They understand that protecting your Big Rocks isn't selfish or unprofessional. It's the only way to sustain excellence over decades, instead of burning bright for a few years and flaming out.

Leading Your Team Differently

One of the first things I like to explain to my team members is that I'm not going to measure their success by the long hours they spend in the office. It's actually the opposite.

Rather than seeing dedication in working long hours, I'm actually going to be inclined to think: why is it taking so long for you to do your work? What do I need to do to help you fix that?

This usually surprises people, especially younger engineers and project managers who've been conditioned to think that face time and endless hours are how you prove yourself.

But I've learned that when someone consistently needs to work 60-hour weeks to keep up with their workload, one of three things is true:

1. They're taking on work that should be delegated or eliminated.

2. They don't have the systems or support they need to work efficiently.

3. We've given them an unrealistic workload.

All three of those are management problems, not dedication problems.

My team certainly has autonomy over their own personal lives, but I also encourage them to consider what's most important. I want them to identify their own Big Rocks and protect them. When people are well-rested, their relationships are healthy, and they have lives outside of work, they make better decisions, catch problems earlier, and bring more creativity to solving challenges.

The best work doesn't come from grinding people into the ground. It comes from creating conditions where people can sustain excellence over the long haul.

Building Systems That Work Without You

Remember those two shutdowns I mentioned in Chapter 3? The ones where I couldn't be on site, so I trusted two of my construction managers to handle everything from the planning, to the coordination and execution?

Everything went perfectly.

That was possible because we'd built systems that didn't require me to be there 24/7. The planning process was documented. The communication protocols were clear. The decision-making framework was established. My construction managers knew what good looked like because we'd built a culture of excellence together.

That's what sustainable leadership looks like—building systems that work even when you're not personally involved.

If your projects only succeed when you work 60-hour weeks, you haven't built a sustainable system, you've built a house of cards, with yourself as the only support beam. When you inevitably burn out, get sick, or need to focus elsewhere, everything collapses.

Again, the goal isn't to make yourself indispensable. It's to make yourself dispensable by developing people and systems that can succeed without you hovering over every decision.

This requires a fundamental shift in how you think about your role. You're not the hero who saves every project through personal sacrifice. You're the shepherd who guides people toward the right goals and the janitor who clears obstacles out of their way so they can do their best work.

The Long Game: Why Sustainable Excellence Matters

Here's what sustainable practices create, whether you're a project engineer just starting out or a director managing programs: When people stay in organizations for decades instead of burning out in five years, institutional knowledge becomes a competitive advantage. Senior project managers remember lessons learned from projects ten years ago. Superintendents have built relationships with medical staff across multiple facilities. Teams know their systems so well they can execute flawlessly without constant supervision.

That knowledge can't be replicated by hiring new people, no matter how talented they are.

If you're early in your career, here's what this means for you: The companies that figure out sustainable workloads aren't just creating better quality of life, they're creating better career trajectories. You'll learn more from senior people who've stuck around than from a revolving door of burned-out managers who leave after five years. You'll build deeper expertise because you're not constantly relearning systems with new leadership. You'll have mentors who actually remember your early projects and can help you grow over time.

If you're leading teams, the business case is clear: retention beats recruitment every time. Well-rested leaders make better decisions. People who aren't constantly fighting fires can actually plan proactively. Teams who trust their leadership will tell you about problems before they become crises.

The return on sustainable practices shows up in:

- Fewer mistakes from exhaustion.

- Stronger client relationships built over years.

- Better problem-solving from institutional knowledge.

- More innovation because people have mental bandwidth to think creatively.

- Career growth that compounds over decades instead of resetting every few years.

Companies that *don't* destroy their people attract the best talent in the industry; those who understand that sustainable excellence beats unsustainable grinding every time.

If you're a young professional watching your peers burn out and leave, you have a choice: find an organization that values sustainability, or become a leader who builds one. Either way, the message is the same—your career is a marathon, not a sprint, and the winners are the ones who pace themselves for the long haul.

How Sustainable Practices Prevent Most Crises

In the next chapter, we're going to go over a major crisis in detail—showing you the step-by-step crisis management process we used when construction debris crashed through a ceiling and landed one foot away from a hospital staff member. It was one of the worst days of my career.

I want you to understand that the way we responded to that crisis—the immediate shutdown, thorough investigation, and systematic rebuilding of trust—all of that was possible because we had capacity.

If I'd been burned out, running on empty, stretched across ten projects with no margin for error, I don't know if we could have handled that crisis as well as we did. The clear thinking required, the emotional resilience to sit through tough meetings, and the energy to implement comprehensive changes. All of that requires having something left in the tank.

Your ability to handle emergencies is directly related to how well you've been taking care of yourself and your team before the crisis hits.

Well-rested leaders make better decisions under pressure. Teams who aren't already burned out have the resilience to work extra hours when it actually matters. Systems that don't rely on one person's heroic effort can absorb shocks without collapsing entirely.

The crisis happened despite our best efforts. But our response worked because we'd built sustainable practices that gave us capacity when we needed it most.

That's the hidden benefit of protecting your Big Rocks and building sustainable systems: you have reserves to draw on when things go wrong. And in healthcare construction, things will go wrong.

The question is whether you'll have anything left to handle it when they do.

Your Next Steps

If you're reading this chapter and recognizing yourself in my CyberKnife story, if you're seeing warning signs you've been ignoring, if you know your current pace isn't sustainable—here's where to start:

This Week:

Identify your Big Rocks. What are the three things that, if you don't have them, your life falls apart? Write them down. Then look at your calendar for this week and honestly assess if these Big Rocks are actually getting protected, or if the sand is filling all your time?

Block time for at least one Big Rock this week. Put it on your calendar like it's a critical meeting—because it is. If your faith matters, schedule worship time. If your family matters, schedule dinner at home with no phone. If your health matters, schedule actual rest, not just sleep.

This Month:

Audit your current workload. Are you consistently working more than 40 hours a week? If so, why? Write down every task you're doing and categorize it: Must be done by me. Could be delegated. Shouldn't be done at all.

Have honest conversations with your team about their workload. Ask them, "What would it take for you to do excellent work without consistently working nights and weekends?" Then actually listen to the answer and address what they tell you.

This Quarter:

Build one system that works without you being personally involved. Document a process. Train someone to handle something you usually control. Create decision-making frameworks that empower others to act independently.

Measure your success differently. Instead of counting hours or projects, start tracking how many people you develop, how many systems you build that don't require heroics, or how many relationships you strengthened instead of depleted.

The goal isn't to work less, it's to work sustainably. The goal isn't to care less, it's to care about the right things in the right order.

Here's what I learned lying in that hospital bed fighting sepsis: the projects will get built whether you destroy yourself or not. The question is whether you'll be around, healthy and whole, to see the impact of the work you've done.

That CyberKnife project we completed two weeks early is still serving patients today. But it's not worth what it cost me—my health, my marriage, years of my life spent grinding when I could have been building something sustainable.

If I could go back and do it differently, I would. I'd still deliver excellence, but I'd do it in a way that didn't require sacrificing everything else that mattered.

You don't have to learn this lesson the way I did. You can make the choice now to protect your Big Rocks, build sustainable systems, lead your team differently, and chase significance instead of just success.

The compound interest of good choices works just as powerfully as the compound interest of bad ones. Small, consistent decisions to protect what matters. Those compound into a career and a life you can actually sustain.

That's not weakness, it's wisdom, and it's the foundation for everything we're going to talk about next—because when crisis inevitably comes, you want to face it with gas in the tank, not running on empty.

Next, let's talk about what happens when, despite your best efforts and sustainable practices, the wheels still fall off.

CHAPTER 6

WHEN THE WHEELS FALL OFF

Leading Through a Crisis

I was sitting in the Planning, Design & Construction field office reviewing change orders with one of my construction managers, going through the pricing line by line, trying to make sense of a particularly complicated change order that had come in earlier that week.

It was late morning. I'd been on site earlier that day for my usual walk-through before heading back to the office a few blocks away for meetings. Nothing was off. Just another Tuesday morning on a complex hospital renovation project.

That's when Sal, the senior project manager from the general contractor, started walking toward me. His face told me something was wrong before he said a word. The construction manager I was working with noticed it too. Our conversation stopped mid-sentence.

Sal walked over to us, his voice low but urgent. "We've got a situation. An accident happened on site. I don't have all the details yet, but I'm hearing that some conduits or pipes fell through the ceiling."

The words hit me like a brick. Shock, then surprise, then that immediate gut-dropping sensation when you know—you just *know*—that everything is about to change.

Conduits don't just fall through ceilings in occupied hospitals. Not unless something went very, very wrong.

"Drop everything," I told Sal. "We're going to the site right now."

Sal and I left the office, nearly running those several blocks faster than we'd ever before. Halfway there, my phone started ringing. Then pinging. Then ringing again.

Each buzz in my pocket was another confirmation that this wasn't going to be good.

Over the next few hours, I'd learn that several four-foot lengths of electrical conduit had crashed through the ceiling of an occupied area, turning into missiles that landed just one foot away from a hospital staff member. One foot. The difference between a dangerous mistake and a tragedy that would have destroyed lives, careers, and everything we'd built at this institution.

This was the worst-case scenario, but we'd planned for it, trained for it, and prayed it would never happen.

All the planning in the world doesn't prepare you for the moment when your phone starts blowing up and you know that how you handle the next few hours will potentially define the rest of your career.

The principles I'd learned about trust, partnership, and transparency—all of it was about to be tested under the kind of pressure that reveals who you really are.

The Walk That Never Ends

Sal and I didn't say much as we walked. What was there to say? At that point, we didn't have the details yet. We didn't know if anyone was hurt. We didn't know the extent of the damage. We didn't even know exactly what had happened.

All we knew was that it was bad.

In construction, especially healthcare construction, there are mistakes you can recover from and mistakes that end careers. There are incidents that become cautionary tales at safety meetings and incidents that make the news. This had all the hallmarks of the latter.

I was trying to think through the immediate priorities: Stop the work. Secure the area. Make sure no one else is in danger. Get the facts. Call Tim. Call Matt.

God, I was going to have to call Matt.

My phone kept buzzing. I glanced at the screen between hurried steps. The superintendent. The safety manager. Someone from facilities. Each notification was another person who'd heard something and wanted answers I didn't have yet.

I silenced the phone and kept walking.

Going through my mind was the fact that we'd built something good at this institution. Over the past several years, I'd gone from outsider consultant to trusted partner to Director of Construction. I'd earned this trust through countless small deposits in the ledger—showing up, keeping promises, protecting their interests, caring about their mission.

As I detailed in Chapter 2, that trust had been built through consistent reliability, transparent communication, and always putting patient safety first. I'd maintained good reporting records, practiced honest billing, and proven time and again that I spent their money like it was my own.

And now, in one moment, all of that trust could be gone.

The question wasn't whether this would damage our relationship—it absolutely would. The question was whether we could rebuild it.

What You Find When You Arrive

The site was already secured when we got there. The superintendent had done exactly what he was supposed to do: stopped all work in the area, evacuated anyone who didn't need to be there, and called for help.

But you could feel the tension. Workers were standing around in small groups, talking in low voices. Safety vests and hard hats were everywhere, but nobody was moving. You could feel an eerie stillness that only happens when something serious has gone wrong and everyone knows it.

I found the superintendent near the affected area. His face was pale.

"Show me," I said.

We suited up—hard hats, safety vests, the usual—and he walked me to where it happened. The ceiling tiles were punctured with holes, debris scattered across the floor. You could see the dents in the floor where the conduits had struck. Four-foot sections of electrical conduit, heavy metal pipes that had been abandoned and tied off loosely with tie wire from a previous project, somehow, came loose and fell straight through the ceiling into an occupied space below.

"Where's the staff member who was nearby?" I asked.

"Shaken up but physically okay, and left for the day," the superintendent said. "She was standing right there." He pointed to a spot about a foot from where one of the conduits had landed.

I've thought about that distance a lot since then. Twelve inches. The difference between "we got lucky" and "lives destroyed."

Standing there looking at the damage, I had two competing thoughts:

First, thank God no one was hurt. Whatever else happens, whatever consequences follow, at least no one was physically injured.

Second, this could have killed someone. The only reason it didn't is pure luck or, if you're a person of faith, which I am, holy intervention. Neither of those is a safety strategy.

The Toughest Phone Calls

I stepped outside to make the calls I'd been dreading since Sal first shared the news.

My first call was to Tim, the Director of Construction who'd become my mentor and boss. He's the man who'd brought me into this institution as a consultant and later, championed my transition to Director of Construction.

"Tim, we've got a serious incident." I kept my voice steady, my words factual. I offered no speculation, I just shared what I knew for certain. "Electrical conduits fell through a ceiling into an occupied space. A staff member was nearby, but not injured. We've stopped work and secured the area. I'm on site now assessing the situation."

Tim's response was immediate and clear. "Keep me updated. I'm notifying Matt and the administration. Do not restart any work until we understand exactly what happened and how to prevent it from happening again. Start an incident report right away."

"Understood."

I was somewhat relieved to know that I wouldn't have to explain what happened to Matt just yet. Tim was a good boss and was willing to buffer me from that while I worked on our plan. Up to this point, my interactions with Matt—the vice president of Planning, Design & Construction—had been limited. Tim handled most of the day-to-day communication with executive leadership. But this wasn't day-to-day. This was crisis-level, and I knew it would pull Matt directly into oversight of our response.

For the rest of the day, I was onsite with the superintendent and the foreman investigating the site on both floors; where the conduits fell from, and the floor where they landed.

By day's end, after I'd pieced together what happened, Matt called and I gave him the same facts I'd given Tim, with no embellishment. When you're delivering bad news, clarity matters more than cushioning the blow.

I recall Matt's first question was, "Did anybody get hurt?"

"Shaken but not injured. The conduit landed about a foot away from where one staff member was standing."

A pause. I could hear him processing that information.

"Mike, I want a full investigation. Root cause analysis. I want to know how this happened and what we're going to do to make absolutely certain it never happens again. You understand what's at stake here?"

"Yes sir. We'll have answers."

"I know you will," he said "Keep me posted." He hung up.

I stood there for a moment, phone in my hand, processing what had just happened. This wasn't a project issue anymore, this was an executive leadership issue. Matt was now directly involved in overseeing our response. That told me everything I needed to know about how seriously the institution was taking this.

Pulling the Big Red Handle

In nuclear power plants, there's an emergency shutdown system called SCRAM. When you pull that handle, everything stops. The reactor shuts down, systems go into safe mode, and nothing restarts until you understand exactly what went wrong and fix it.

Standing on that job site, looking at the debris on the floor and the holes in the ceiling, I knew we needed to pull our own version of that handle.

"All work in this area stops," I told the superintendent. "I want this floor and the floor above completely shut down until we know what happened."

The superintendent nodded, having already started the process. Hearing it confirmed from me made it official.

"Our workers who were involved—where are they?"

"Sent home. They've been told not to return to this site."

That decision had already been made, and it was the right one. We didn't even know whose fault this was, if anyone's, but keeping them on site while emotions were running high wouldn't help the situation.

In crisis management, the immediate response matters more than almost anything else. You can recover from a lot of mistakes, but you can't recover from failing to take decisive action when safety is compromised.

When patient safety is at stake, especially in a situation where lives could have been lost, you don't worry about project timelines or budget impacts. You stop everything and figure out what went wrong.

The superintendent and I walked the site methodically, documenting everything. We took photos of the damage and measurements of where the conduits landed. We recorded meticulous notes about who was in the area, what work was happening, and what the conditions were like.

Every detail mattered because we were going to have to explain this to a lot of people, including institutional administration, safety officials, potentially regulatory agencies, and certainly the hospital staff who worked in this building every day.

They deserved answers. More than that—they deserved to know this would never happen again.

The Investigation: No Excuses, Just Facts

The next several days were consumed by investigation. We interviewed everyone involved, from the workers who'd been on the floor above, to the superintendent, the foreman, and anyone who had any information about how this work was being done.

We reviewed the drawings. We examined the work plan and the safety protocols that should have been in place.

Slowly, the picture became clear.

The conduits had been cut off and abandoned on the floor above. The workers were going through and demoing debris and old infrastructure to make room for the new electrical and HVAC systems. We found that a previous project in that same area had left many four-foot lengths of conduit loosely secured with tie wire. Two laborers, not realizing that these conduits were not secured to anything else, cut the tie wire. Two conduits fell to the floor below before they realized what was happening. The rest remained suspended, for now. We needed to devise a plan to safely remove them.

Through a combination of miscommunication, inadequate supervision, and workers not fully understanding the importance of the securing process, those conduits had been left loose.

This was a series of small failures that compounded into a near-catastrophe. That's how most accidents happen. It's rarely one massive mistake, rather it's through several small mistakes that happen to line up in exactly the wrong way.

During the investigation, we didn't make excuses. We didn't blame the workers. We didn't point fingers at the GC or the subcontractors. We didn't try to minimize what happened or shift responsibility.

The whole team owned it.

Every meeting, report, and conversation started with the acknowledgment that this happened on our watch, under our oversight, and we were responsible for making sure it never happened again.

That's what accountability looks like. There was no finger-pointing or blame-shifting. There was just clear-eyed ownership of the problem and a commitment to the solution.

The Meetings: Listening Without Defensiveness

Over the next month, I sat through more meetings about this incident than I could count.

Meetings with hospital administration, the safety committee, department heads of staff who worked in the affected area, the risk management team, and even Matt and Tim— every single one of them started with someone explaining how bad this could have been, as if we didn't already know.

"Do you realize that conduit could have killed someone?"

Yes. We realized.

"Do you understand the impact this has on staff morale and sense of safety?"

Yes. We understood.

"What assurances can you give us that this won't happen again?"

That was the question that really mattered. That's the one we needed to answer, not with words, but with action.

Those meetings taught me that crisis management is about listening. It's not about defending yourself or making promises it won't happen again. It's about rReally listening to what people have to say.

Listen when people are angry. Listen when they're saying things you've already heard ten times. Listen even when you want to interrupt and explain and justify.

You sit there and you listen because they need to say it. The hospital staff needed to express their fear and frustration. The administrators needed to make clear how seriously they took this. The safety committee needed to go through every detail to understand what happened.

We needed to hear all of it, and do so without defensiveness, because that's how you rebuild trust after a massive withdrawal from the ledger.

In Chapter 2, I outlined the protocol for rebuilding trust, including four phases: Immediate Response, Investigation and Analysis, Implementation and Proof, and Validation and Moving Forward. This is what Phase 2 looks like in practice—sitting through difficult conversations and accepting increased oversight without complaint.

Some of those meetings were brutal. I'd walk out emotionally exhausted, having spent two hours hearing about all the ways we'd failed, but I never once thought "this isn't fair" or "they're overreacting."

They weren't overreacting. If anything, they were showing remarkable restraint. We'd had a near-miss that could have killed one of their colleagues, and they had every right to be angry and scared, demanding answers.

Our job was to give them those answers and prove—through action more than words—that we'd learned from this.

The Long Road Back

The first step was to safely remove any more of these abandoned conduits. While the main project was on hold, several phases of conduit removal were scheduled. It all had to be done at odd hours because it was all directly above occupied spaces.

The policy changes that came out of this incident were comprehensive and, frankly, should have been in place from the beginning.

We instituted new protocols for overhead work in occupied areas. We added mandatory secondary checks before starting any work that could create falling hazards. We added enhanced supervision requirements, additional safety training, physical barriers and warning systems.

Writing new policies was the easy part. The challenge was implementing them consistently, day after day, until they became habits instead of requirements.

That took time.

It took about a month before we were allowed to restart work in the affected area. The investigation gave us answers within the first week. The rest of that time was spent rebuilding trust, a task that required demonstrating real change, because saying you'll do something is never as good as doing it.

Every day, we submitted detailed reports on our safety improvements. We documented our training sessions. We showed the physical changes we were making to prevent similar incidents.

We invited hospital leadership to inspect our new protocols. We welcomed their questions and scrutiny. We made ourselves accountable not just to our own standards, but to theirs.

Slowly, the trust started to rebuild.

The first sign came when Matt stopped asking for daily updates and moved to weekly. That told me he was regaining confidence that we had control of the situation.

Another sign came a few months later when Tim called me into his office, telling me,

"The project's back on track. More importantly, the safety culture is very much improved. Leadership is satisfied with your response."

I didn't know what to say to that. I still felt the weight of what could have happened, what almost happened.

"Mike, everyone makes mistakes," Tim continued. "What separates good leaders from mediocre ones is what they do after the mistake. You did everything right. You owned it, you fixed it, and you made the team better because of it."

Good Scars: What Crisis Teaches You

Here's the paradox: that falling conduit incident created the strongest safety culture this institution had ever had.

Before the incident, safety was something we talked about. After the incident, it became something we lived.

Those new protocols we implemented became the standard for every contractor who worked at this medical center. The training we developed got rolled out system-wide. The lessons we learned prevented countless other potential incidents.

That's what I call a "good scar." The injury hurt like hell when it happened. The healing took time and left a mark, but it made us stronger in that exact spot.

The safety policies that came out of this crisis became the model that other hospitals asked us about. When contractors interviewed to work at this institution, our safety requirements became the selling point, not a burden.

And paradoxically, my relationship with Matt—which I'd thought might be destroyed by this incident—actually became stronger. He saw how we responded when everything went wrong. He saw us take full responsibility, implement real changes and follow through on every commitment. He saw that we cared more about doing the right thing than protecting our reputation.

That crisis became the foundation for a different kind of trust. We were going to make mistakes again, but we earned the trust that when we did, we'd handle them with integrity.

A few months after we'd restarted work, Matt pulled me aside after a meeting to say, "You handled that right. The team owned it completely. That matters."

The proof that these lessons stuck with me came years later, when I was working on a different project for a different client. I was walking the site during plumbing rough-in work when I noticed something that made my blood run cold: open cores in the deck. Holes cut through the floor with nothing securing them, nothing preventing something—or someone—from falling through.

Based on that hellish experience with the falling conduits, I didn't hesitate. I stopped the project immediately, pulled the superintendent aside, and made it clear that nothing moves forward until proper core safety is implemented. That needed to include barriers, signage, secondary checks…the whole protocol.

Now, I don't know for certain if stopping that work prevented another crisis. What I do know is that one didn't happen. The lesson about overhead hazards and the importance of securing anything that could fall was knowledge embedded into how I looked at job sites from that day forward.

I like to think that somewhere along the way, that heightened awareness and willingness to pull the emergency brake probably did prevent another tragedy. That's what good scars do—they make you see dangers you might have walked past before.

What Crisis Actually Tests

Looking back on that falling conduit incident, I can see what was really being tested.

It wasn't our safety protocols—those clearly had gaps, which is why the accident happened in the first place.

It wasn't our technical expertise—we knew how to secure conduits properly. Knowledge wasn't the problem.

We were being tested on everything I'd talked about in the previous chapters:

The Foundation (Chapter 1): Were we truly transformational partners, or just transactional contractors pretending to care? The crisis forced us to prove which one we were.

The Currency of Trust (Chapter 2): Did we have enough deposits in the trust ledger to survive a massive withdrawal? Could we rebuild that trust through transparency rather than perfection?

The Internal Team (Chapter 3): Did we have the kind of team that could handle brutal honesty and provide unwavering support when everything went wrong? Could we check our egos and focus on solutions?

External Partnerships (Chapter 4): Would our design and construction partners stand with us or distance themselves when the crisis hit? (They stood with us, which told me we'd built real partnerships.)

Sustainable Excellence (Chapter 5): Were we able to handle the crisis because we'd built sustainable practices that gave us capacity when we needed it most, or were we already running on empty when disaster struck?

The answer to all those questions determined whether we survived this crisis or were destroyed by it.

It was from situations like this where I learned that you don't build crisis management skills during a crisis. You build them beforehand, through all the small daily disciplines, the trust deposits, the team development, the sustainable practices.

When the conduit fell through that ceiling, we didn't suddenly become better leaders. We just revealed what kind of leaders we already were. The only reason we passed that test was because we'd been preparing for it—unknowingly—through every decision we'd made before that terrible Tuesday morning.

When Everything Goes Wrong: Your Crisis Playbook

I can't tell you how to prevent every crisis. Accidents happen. Mistakes occur. Systems fail.

But I can tell you how to respond when they do, based on what worked for us:

Hour One: Stop Everything and Get the Facts

- Secure the area immediately.

- Make sure no one else is in danger.

- Get basic facts before you start making calls.

- Don't speculate, don't minimize, don't spin.

When I arrived on site, I didn't start making excuses or theorizing about what happened. I focused on three things: Is everyone safe? What do we know for certain? What needs to happen right now to prevent further harm?

Hour Two: Make the Hard Calls

- Notify leadership immediately with facts, not theories.

- Take ownership without waiting to be asked.

- Commit to a full investigation and real solutions.

- Don't make promises you can't keep.

My calls with Tim and Matt were brief and factual. I didn't try to soften the blow or predict outcomes I couldn't guarantee. I told them what I knew, what we were doing, and what we'd committed to figure out.

Day One: Begin the Investigation

- Bring in qualified experts if needed.

- Interview everyone involved.

- Document everything.

- Look for root causes, not scapegoats.

We didn't rush the investigation to get back to work faster. We took the time to understand exactly what happened and why. Every interview was documented. Every photo was cataloged. Every detail mattered because we needed to understand the full picture, not just the obvious surface cause.

Week One: Develop the Response

- Identify specific failures and gaps.

- Create concrete corrective actions.

- Don't just patch the symptom, fix the system.

- Prepare to be held accountable.

The new protocols we developed weren't just about preventing more conduits from falling. They were about creating a system of checks and supervision that would catch any similar hazard before it became dangerous. We went deeper than the immediate cause to address the underlying gaps.

Month One: Prove You've Changed

Implement new protocols consistently.

Welcome oversight and scrutiny.

Report progress without being asked.

Accept that rebuilding trust takes time.

Every day for a month, we submitted detailed safety reports. We didn't wait for them to ask—we proactively showed them what we were doing. When they wanted to inspect our new procedures, we welcomed it as an opportunity to demonstrate our commitment.

Going Forward: Make It Mean Something

- Turn crisis lessons into permanent improvements.
- Share what you learned with others.
- Create "good scars" that make you stronger.
- Remember what almost happened, even when things are going well.

Years later, I still think about that one foot of distance. I still use that incident as a teaching example when training new teams. I still check overhead work areas with extra scrutiny. The scar reminds me that patient safety isn't theoretical, it's one foot between a near-miss and a tragedy.

What This Means for You

You might never have conduits fall through a ceiling. Your crisis might look completely different.

But I can promise that if you work in construction long enough, something will go seriously wrong. A safety incident. A major delay. A relationship destroyed. Something that tests everything you've built.

When that moment comes, these questions will determine whether you survive it:

- Have you built enough trust to absorb a major withdrawal from the ledger?

- Do you have the character to own your mistakes without excuses?

- Is your team strong enough to be brutally honest while supporting each other?

- Have you built sustainable practices that give you capacity for crisis?

- Can you listen to angry people without becoming defensive?

- Are you willing to accept increased oversight and scrutiny as the price of rebuilding trust?

- Will you implement real changes or just temporary fixes?

Those aren't theoretical questions. They're the ones I had to answer in real-time, under pressure, with careers and relationships on the line.

The falling conduit crisis was the worst day of my tenure at that institution. It was also the moment that defined what kind of leader I actually was, not what kind I aspired to be.

I hope you never face something that serious. But if you do, I hope you've built the foundation to handle it the right way—with integrity, accountability, and unwavering commitment to making things right.

That's what separates leaders who destroy trust during a crisis from leaders who somehow, against all odds, end up building it stronger than before.

Your Next Steps

You can't plan for every crisis, but you can prepare for how you'll respond:

This Week:

- Review your current project for potential safety hazards you've been minimizing or ignoring.

- Have a conversation with your team about what you'd do if something went seriously wrong.

- Make sure you have clear escalation procedures for emergencies.

This Month:

- Audit your safety protocols honestly.

- Ensure JHAs and MOPs are being completed thoughtfully and reviewed properly.

- Add "Upcoming Risk Activities" as a standing agenda item in OAC meetings.

- Identify the "near misses" on your current project and address them before they become real incidents.

- Practice delivering bad news clearly and owning problems without excuses.

This Quarter:

- Build your trust ledger through consistent small deposits so you have capital if you need it.

- Develop your team's capacity to handle difficult conversations without defensiveness.

- Create sustainable practices that give you reserves for crisis response.

I'm not trying to make you paranoid that something catastrophic is imminent. The goal is to build the character, systems, and relationships that will allow you to handle it well when it inevitably happens.

In healthcare construction, patient safety is always at stake. When something goes wrong, the quality of your response will define your career far more than the mistake itself.

That conduit landed one foot away from a hospital staff member. I think about that distance often. It reminds me that we're not just building buildings—we're building in spaces where people's lives depend on us getting it right.

When we get it wrong, we owe it to them to own it completely, fix it thoroughly, and make damn sure it never happens again.

That's not just crisis management. That's the basic requirement for anyone who builds where lives are saved.

CHAPTER 7

ESSENTIAL SKILLS FOR DAILY SUCCESS

Alright, we've spent the last six chapters talking about the big ideas: trust, partnership, mission, and not grinding yourself into dust. That's the "why." This chapter is the "how."

This is the unsexy, nuts-and-bolts stuff that makes all that high-minded thinking actually work. It's the blocking and tackling of construction. Get this right, and you have a foundation for everything else. Get it wrong, and the prettiest mission statement in the world won't save your project.

I'm not going to give you step-by-step instructions on every technical process—that would turn this book into a thousand-page manual that nobody would actually read. What I will give you is perspective on the skills and processes that matter most, what people typically get wrong, and how to think about these fundamentals in a way that serves the mission-driven approach we've been building.

Think of this as your field guide to the daily job. If you've been in the business for a while, some of this will be a review. If you're just starting out, most of this could be new. Either way, this is the foundation that everything else sits on.

When Marcus, my superintendent at that Southern California hospital, took me to lunch and told me the MRI project went perfectly, it was because we mastered the basics you're about to read about. We had the right contract structure. We handled the paperwork—submittals, RFIs, change orders—with discipline and speed. We planned the work methodically and showed up every day ready to execute. The transformational partnership I talked about in Chapter 1 only worked because the fundamentals were solid.

That's what this chapter is about—the foundational skills that let everything else happen.

Some of it might seem basic, and none of it is glamorous. But I promise you, the best leaders I know are masters of these fundamentals. They do sweat the small stuff, so they don't have to sweat the big stuff later.

One more thing before we dive in: this chapter speaks to different audiences depending on the topic, which makes it longer than any other chapter in the book. Some sections are written for owners and their representatives—the people hiring and overseeing contractors. Other sections speak directly to contractors doing the work. And some apply to both. I'll label each section, to make the chapter easier to navigate, and make it clear who I'm talking to as we go.

Let's get into it.

Section 7.1: Before You Break Ground - The Precon Phase

What Precon Actually Is (And When It's Worth It)

Preconstruction—or precon—is the phase before you sign a construction contract where you're figuring out what the project will actually cost, how long it will take, and whether the design is even buildable.

Most people think precon is just about pricing. It's not. Good precon is about risk identification and mitigation; it's about finding the problems while they're still cheap to fix…on paper instead of in the field.

In healthcare construction, precon becomes even more critical because you're often building in an occupied facility where mistakes can impact patient care. The time you invest upfront in understanding phasing, infection control requirements, utility shutdowns, and operational constraints will save you exponentially more time and money during construction.

Not every project needs formal precon. Small, straightforward projects with complete documents can go straight to bid. But complex renovations in occupied hospitals? You want precon. The investment pays for itself in avoided change orders and schedule delays.

Throughout my career in California, I worked on many projects that I came to call "trifectas"—large-scale construction in an occupied facility, under OSHPD jurisdiction, and requiring complex phasing. If you've never dealt with OSHPD—California's Office of Statewide Health Planning and Development—consider yourself lucky. It's one of the most rigorous regulatory environments in the country, with seismic and life-safety requirements that can turn straightforward projects into coordination nightmares.

These trifecta projects absolutely benefit from a formal precon phase with an experienced design team and a design-assist contractor involved early. This is imperative, because you need the architect and engineers thinking about constructability while they're still drawing. You need the contractor identifying phasing conflicts before they're locked into the permit documents. And you need everyone coordinating on how to build seismically-compliant systems in tight existing conditions without shutting down patient care.

I've watched projects that skipped precon on trifecta work, and the pattern is always the same: the contractor discovers conflicts during construction that should have been caught in design. The hospital discovers operational impacts that weren't properly planned for. OSHPD inspectors find issues that require expensive redesigns. The budget bleeds, the schedule slips, and everyone points fingers.

Compare that to trifecta projects where we invested in proper precon: the contractor walks the existing conditions with the design team during schematic design. They model the phasing scenarios together. They coordinate the seismic details before the submittal to OSHPD. They develop realistic schedules based on what can actually be built in an occupied facility. Yes, precon costs money upfront—but it saves multiples of that investment by catching problems while they're still just lines on a drawing.

How to Run RFQs and RFPs That Attract the Right Partners

A Request for Qualifications (RFQ) asks, "Are you capable of doing this work?" A Request for Proposals (RFP) asks, "How would you approach this work and what will it cost?"

The mistake most owners make is treating these as box-checking exercises. They write vague scopes, set unrealistic timelines for responses, and wonder why they get lowest-common-denominator proposals from contractors who are just throwing darts at numbers.

The truth is, good contractors are busy. If your RFQ or RFP looks like every other commodity bid, you'll attract commodity contractors. If you want partners who understand healthcare construction, you need to ask questions that reveal their experience and approach.

Instead of "Describe your relevant experience," ask, "Describe a time when you had to modify your construction approach to accommodate patient care operations. What did you learn?"

Instead of just requesting a price, ask how they plan to phase the work, what their infection control protocols are, and how they'll handle emergencies in an occupied facility.

The quality of your questions determines the quality of their responses. If you ask commodity questions, you'll get commodity answers.

Choosing the Right Contract Type for Your Project

There are several contract delivery methods you'll encounter in healthcare construction, each with different risk allocations and relationship structures.

Lump Sum (Fixed Price) works when you have complete, detailed documents and minimal risk of changes. The contractor carries the risk of cost overruns, so they'll price in that risk. If you have a simple project with finished design, this can work well. But in healthcare construction, with its complexities and occupied facility challenges, true lump sum contracts are rare.

Cost Plus (Time and Materials) gives you maximum flexibility but minimum cost certainty. The contractor is reimbursed for actual costs plus a fee. This works for projects where scope is uncertain or you need to start fast before design is complete. But it requires trust and excellent oversight because the contractor has less incentive to control costs.

Construction Manager at Risk with GMP is probably the most common delivery method for complex healthcare projects, and for good reason. Here's how it works: you bring the construction manager on board during design—sometimes at schematic design, sometimes earlier. They provide cost estimates, constructability reviews, and help refine the design based on budget realities. Once design reaches a certain completion level (usually 90-100%), they commit to a Guaranteed Maximum Price.

The beauty of CM at Risk is that you get contractor input when it matters most—during design—but you still have cost certainty before you break ground. The contractor is incentivized to keep costs down because they absorb overruns above the GMP, but they can also share in savings if the project comes in under budget.

The key to making CM at Risk work is bringing the contractor in early enough that their input actually matters. If you wait until design is 95 percent% complete, you've missed most of the value. Bring them in at schematic design or earlier, and they can help you avoid expensive mistakes before they're locked into the drawings.

Design-Build takes it a step further by putting design and construction under one contract. You hire a design-build entity (usually led by either a contractor or an architect) who is responsible for both designing and building the project.

The advantage is single-point accountability. No finger-pointing between designer and builder because they're the same entity. Decision-making can be faster, and the integration of design and construction expertise from day one often leads to better constructability and value.

The disadvantage is less owner control over design. You're trusting the design-build team to balance your needs with their desire to build efficiently. This requires a very clear scope and performance criteria upfront, plus strong owner representation to ensure design quality doesn't get sacrificed for construction convenience.

Design-build works well for projects with clear functional requirements but where you're open to different design solutions. It's less ideal when you have very specific design expectations or when the program is still evolving. Equipment replacement projects are a good fit for design build agreements as long as you have experienced architects, engineers, and contractors that make up the design build team familiar with the equipment and control rooms.

Integrated Project Delivery (IPD) is the most collaborative—and least common—delivery method. In true IPD, owner, architect, and contractor enter into a single multiparty agreement. Everyone shares risk and reward. The team makes decisions collaboratively, and financial incentives are aligned around project success rather than individual profit.

IPD requires a level of trust and transparency that makes most traditional construction players uncomfortable. Everyone's books are open. Profits are shared based on project outcomes, not individual company performance. It's collaborative in a way that feels radical in an industry built on adversarial relationships.

When IPD works, it's remarkable. The alignment of incentives means everyone is genuinely focused on the best outcome for the project. Problems get solved collaboratively instead of turning into claims. Innovation flourishes because people aren't protecting their piece of the pie.

But IPD requires the right team and the right culture. If any party comes in with a traditional adversarial mindset, the whole thing falls apart. You need people who are willing to be genuinely transparent about costs, who will make decisions based on what's best for the project rather than what's best for their company, and who can handle the discomfort of shared risk.

I've seen IPD work beautifully on complex healthcare projects where the owner, design team, and contractors were all committed to the collaborative approach. I've also seen it fail spectacularly when one party wasn't truly bought in and reverted to traditional behavior of protecting their interests.

Here's what matters more than the delivery method: the quality of the relationship and the clarity of expectations. I've seen good projects with all of these methods and disasters with all of them as well. The contract structure creates the framework, but the partnership determines the outcome.

Choose your delivery method based on:

- How complete your design is when you need to start.
- How much cost certainty you need upfront.
- How much you value contractor input during design.
- The complexity of the project and level of coordination required.
- Whether you have the right partners who can handle the chosen approach.

The wrong delivery method with the right partners will probably work out fine. The right delivery method with the wrong partners will definitely fail.

Bid Leveling: Making Sure You're Comparing Apples to Apples

You get three bids back. One is $10 million, one is $12 million, one is $15 million. Easy choice, right? Take the low bid?

Not so fast.

Bid leveling is the process of making sure all bidders are actually pricing the same scope of work. It's tedious work, but it's essential.

The $10 million bid might be excluding temporary utilities that the other bidders included. The $12 million bid might include an allowance for unforeseen conditions that the low bidder ignored. The $15 million bid might be the only one that properly accounted for the infection control requirements.

You need to go line by line through each proposal and identify what's included, what's excluded, and what's different. Create a spreadsheet that normalizes the bids by adding back exclusions or removing over-pricing. Only then can you make an informed decision.

Bid leveling is about snuffing out the liars. If one bid is 20 percent lower than everyone else's, they either missed something big or they're planning to make it all back on change orders. That's a red flag, not a bargain.

Remember that contractor I talked about in Chapter 2 who specialized in bidding projects with incomplete documents, then change-ordering them to death? He consistently came in as the low bidder. And twice, I fell for it. The first time, shame on him. The second time, shame on me. After that, he never worked at that hospital system again.

That's the pattern to watch for: the contractor who's always the low bid but never the low final cost. Bid leveling helps you catch them before they catch you.

The low bid is rarely the best value. The bid that most accurately reflects the actual scope of work usually is.

What Value Engineering Really Means (Versus What It's Become)

True value engineering is finding ways to achieve the same or better performance at lower cost. It's creative problem-solving that makes the project better and cheaper.

In many cases, however, value engineering has become nothing more than cost-cutting dressed up with a fancy name. "Value engineering" that sacrifices quality, durability, or functionality isn't value engineering—it's just cheapening the project.

Real value engineering happens during design, when still you have options. Can we use a different mechanical system that achieves the same performance at lower first cost and operating cost? Can we simplify the structural system without compromising strength? Can we phase the work differently to reduce the impact on operations?

Fake value engineering happens when someone realizes the project is over budget and starts cutting things to make the numbers work. That's not engineering—that's panic.

If someone proposes "value engineering" that reduces quality or performance, push back. Ask, "How does this maintain or improve the original intent?" If they can't answer that question convincingly, it's not value engineering.

Section 7.2: The Build - Managing Construction in Occupied Hospitals

This is about the daily grind of construction in an occupied healthcare facility. The core message here is simple: your project is a guest in someone else's house, only it's a house where lives are on the line. You don't get to act like you own the place.

Everything in this section comes back to the principle that patient care doesn't stop for your construction schedule. Ever. Your job is to figure out how to build without interfering with the primary mission of saving lives.

Change Order Review and Negotiation

If you're the owner or owner's rep reviewing change orders, this section is for you. But contractors should still read it too. Understanding what the other side is looking for makes the whole process work better.

To put it plainly, change orders are where relationships go to die. But they don't have to.

The reality is, changes happen on every project. Unforeseen conditions arise. Design clarifications are needed. Owner-requested modifications slow things down. The question isn't whether you'll have change orders—it's whether you'll handle them with transparency, or turn them into trench warfare.

When a contractor hands you a change order, look at the final number, then ask for the backup. See the timecards, the material invoices, the subcontractor quotes. (For large change orders, three sub proposals are industry standard.) My approach was always to treat it like a puzzle, not a fight. "Help me understand how you got to this number."

When you show you're willing to pay for legitimate costs but need to see the math, it changes the conversation from an argument to an accounting exercise. Most contractors appreciate that approach because they know you're not trying to nickel-and-dime them—you're just trying to understand what you're paying for.

Another critical question is if this change is a true add, or is the change replacing something the contract already purchased? I can't tell you how many times I've caught contractors trying to charge for work that was already in their scope, just executed differently. They're not always trying to scam you—sometimes they genuinely don't realize they're double-dipping. But it's your job to catch it.

The best change order negotiations I've had were the ones where we sat down together, looked at the drawings, looked at the costs, and figured out what was fair. The worst ones were where someone decided to take a position and defend it regardless of the facts.

Transparency is the key. If the contractor shows you their actual costs and explains their reasoning, you can usually find common ground. If they just throw a number at you and expect you to accept it, that's when trust starts eroding.

Planning and Executing Large Shutdowns

Whether you're the contractor planning the work or the owner's rep overseeing it, shutdowns require the same level of precision from everyone involved.

Think of a shutdown in an occupied hospital as a medical procedure on the building. You need the same level of precision the doctors and nurses have with their patients. The phrase "oops" is not an option.

Remember those two simultaneous shutdowns I mentioned in Chapter 3? My construction managers pulled off two major shutdowns in one weekend without me even being there because we did the painstaking, boring, essential planning work for weeks leading up to that day.

Most people think the hard part of a shutdown is the execution. It's not. The hard part is the planning.

Months before shutdown day, you need to start the investigative work.

- What circuits are you shutting down?

- What equipment is on those circuits?

- What's the backup plan for each piece of critical equipment?

- Who needs to be notified? What's the sequence of shutdown and restart?

- What could go wrong, and what's your contingency for each scenario?

This isn't work you can delegate to someone who doesn't understand hospital operations. You need people who can translate between construction language and medical language. When the electrician says, "We're shutting down panel 3A," you need to be able to tell the nursing staff, "This affects the emergency power outlets in rooms 401-408, so here's how we're handling your life-support equipment while the power to those rooms is down."

The investigation phase requires walking the affected areas with both construction and medical staff. You're looking for things that aren't on any drawing—the piece of equipment someone plugged in five years ago that nobody remembered to document, the critical system that's labeled wrong on the panel, or the workaround that became permanent.

Once you understand exactly what you're affecting, you develop the Method of Procedure—the step-by-step playbook for how the shutdown will happen. We'll talk more about MOPs in a minute, but for shutdowns, this document is your bible.

Then comes the coordination meetings. Not one meeting—multiple meetings with different stakeholders. The facilities team needs to understand the technical details. The medical staff needs to understand the impact on patients. The administration needs to understand the risk and the mitigation plan. Security needs to know what's happening in case of emergency. You're essentially building consensus that this risky thing needs to happen, and you've planned it well enough to minimize that risk.

The execution on shutdown day should be almost boring if you've done the planning right. Everyone knows their role. Every step is documented. Every contingency is planned for. You're just executing a plan that's been reviewed and refined dozens of times.

The thing about shutdowns is that something will always go wrong. You find that a breaker that was supposed to control one panel actually controls two, or a backup generator that was tested last month doesn't start this time. Perhaps a piece of equipment that was supposed to be on normal power is actually on emergency power.

That's why the planning includes contingencies for every step. When something goes wrong—and it will—you don't panic. You execute the contingency plan.

The two shutdowns my construction managers handled without me worked perfectly because we'd planned for everything that could go wrong. When a minor issue came up, they already knew how to handle it. They didn't need to call me because the MOP had the answer.

That's what good planning looks like. The day of execution should be the easiest part of the whole process.

When You Need an MOP and What Makes a Good One

This applies to everyone—contractors creating MOPs and owners reviewing them.

A Method of Procedure—MOP—is your step-by-step playbook for any activity that could impact patient care or hospital operations.

You need an MOP anytime your work could affect:

- Power to patient care areas
- Medical gas systems
- HVAC serving occupied spaces
- Water supply to critical areas
- Fire protection systems
- Any system where failure could impact patient safety

Period. No exceptions.

The problem with most MOPs is that they're either too long or too vague. I've seen 50-page binders that nobody reads and I've seen one-page "MOPs" that don't actually tell you anything useful.

A good MOP is simple and specific:

Who is doing the work? Not just "the contractor"—actual names and phone numbers.

What exactly is happening? Step by step, in sequence, with no assumptions.

When is each step occurring? With specific times, not "in the morning."

What is the backup plan if something goes wrong? Note that for each critical step.

Who do you call if there's a problem? Include multiple contact numbers.

It should be so clear that a new person could walk in, read it, and understand the plan. If you need tribal knowledge to interpret your MOP, it's not a good MOP.

The best MOPs I've seen include simple diagrams showing what's being shut down, what stays energized, and where the critical equipment is located. Visual information cuts through a lot of confusion.

The MOP needs to be reviewed and approved by the hospital before you execute it. That's a requirement that should be obvious, but it often isn't. This review and approval cannot happen the day before, it should be weeks before. The hospital staff needs time to verify your information, identify things you missed, and coordinate with their staff.

A thorough and organized MOP is a communication tool that ensures everyone understands the risk and the mitigation plan.

Phasing Plans That Actually Work in Occupied Spaces

This is primarily for design teams and contractors creating phasing plans, but owners need to know what to look for when reviewing them.

A phasing plan that looks pretty on paper but doesn't account for how nurses actually get from the med room to a patient's room is worthless.

The test for any phasing plan is simple: Can the people who work there still do their jobs effectively? Not theoretically—actually.

I've seen beautiful phasing plans that completely blocked critical circulation paths. I've seen plans that forced nursing staff to walk an extra five minutes every time they needed to reach a patient—which might not sound like much until you realize they're making that trip dozens of times per shift, and every minute they're walking is a minute they're not providing patient care.

Before you finalize any phasing plan, walk the route with the head nurse of that department. Looking at drawings in a conference room can only tell you so much. Actually walk with them in the space and them, "What about this plan is going to make your day harder?"

Their answer will be more valuable than a dozen meetings with architects.

Pay attention to things like:

- Where do they need to bring equipment? Can they still get large beds, crash carts, or portable X-ray machines through your barriers?

- Where are the emergency exits? Can you maintain egress even with construction walls in place?

- What are the sight lines? Can staff at the nurses' station still see patient room doors?

- Where are they storing supplies now? If you're blocking that storage room, where will those supplies go?

The goal isn't to make their day easier—that's impossible during construction. The goal is to not make it unnecessarily harder.

Good phasing plans are developed collaboratively with the people who actually use the space. Bad phasing plans are developed in isolation by people who've never worked a shift in a hospital.

Infection Control Essentials (ICRA)

For contractors: this is how you execute infection control. For owners: this is what to expect and verify.

This is non-negotiable. Construction dust is a mess, but for an immunocompromised patient, it can be a death sentence. You have to treat the air in your construction zone like it's poison, because for some patients, it is.

ICRA stands for Infection Control Risk Assessment. It's the process of evaluating what risk your construction activities pose to patients and what measures you need to take to mitigate that risk.

The basics are straightforward but require discipline:

Negative air machines: These create negative pressure in your construction zone so that dust and particles can't escape into occupied areas. The air gets filtered before it's exhausted. You maintain this negative pressure 24/7 while you're working; during demo especially, but any time the barrier is breached.

Hard barriers: Plastic sheeting might be fine for your basement renovation at home. In a hospital, you build actual walls—typically metal studs and drywall—to contain the construction area. These barriers need to be airtight. Any penetrations get sealed. Doors are airlocks with sticky mats.

Sticky mats: These adhesive mats at every entrance and exit capture dust from boots before it gets tracked into clean areas. Replace them regularly.

Air monitoring: Depending on the risk level, you may need to continuously monitor particle counts to ensure your containment is working.

Cleaning protocols: Before you open a barrier to occupied space, you clean. Then you clean again. Then the hospital inspects and approves. You don't tear down barriers on your schedule—you tear down when the hospital says it's safe.

The level of infection control required depends on the type of construction and the patient population nearby. Demo work near immunocompromised patients requires the highest level of protection. Painting in an area away from patient care might require minimal measures.

You don't get to decide what level is appropriate. The hospital's infection control team makes that call based on their risk assessment. Your job is to execute their requirements flawlessly.

I've seen contractors try to cut corners on infection control because "the patients are on the other side of the building" or "it's just a small amount of dust." That's not acceptable. The infection control protocols exist because we're building in spaces where vulnerable people are trying to heal. Their safety is more important than the project's convenience or schedule.

Project Inspections and Inspectors

For contractors: here's how to work with inspectors. For owners: here's what to expect from the inspection process.

Inspections are how you verify that the work meets the standards— building codes, contract requirements, and hospital-specific needs.

You'll deal with several types of inspectors:

Building inspectors from the local jurisdiction to verify code compliance. These are the official inspections required for permits. You can't skip them, you can't rush them, and you need to respect them. Good building inspectors catch problems before they become disasters.

Hospital inspectors—usually facilities staff or specialized consultants—verify that the work meets the hospital's operational requirements. They're checking things the building inspector doesn't care about but matter enormously for hospital operations. Are the ceiling tiles the right type for a patient care area? Is the flooring properly sealed? Does the door swing meet their infection control requirements?

Third-party inspectors—sometimes required for specialized systems like medical gas, fire protection, or complex MEP systems. These inspectors bring specialized expertise and often need to certify systems before they can be commissioned.

Your job is to make their job easy. That means:

- Scheduling inspections with adequate notice.
- Having the right work ready when they show up.
- Providing documentation they need.
- Fixing problems they identify promptly.

The contractors who fight with inspectors or try to hide problems make their own lives harder. The inspectors are going to find the issues eventually—better to address them proactively than to have them discovered at final inspection when they'll delay your occupancy.

Treat inspectors as partners in ensuring quality, not adversaries trying to slow you down.

Running OAC Meetings That Add Value

This section is primarily for whoever runs these meetings—usually the owner's rep or the general contractor—but everyone who attends should understand what makes them effective.

Most Owner-Architect-Contractor (OAC) meetings are a colossal waste of time. They're just a recap of things everyone already knows or can read in a report.

Here's how they usually go: The contractor presents a schedule update everyone already reviewed via email. The architect mentions some RFIs that are already being processed. The owner asks a question that could have been answered in two minutes outside the meeting. An hour later, everyone leaves having accomplished nothing that couldn't have been handled more efficiently in writing.

Your OAC meeting should be forward-looking. Spend 10 percent of the time on what happened last week and 90 percent on what's happening in the next two weeks.

The questions that matter:

- What are the roadblocks to progress?
- Where do we need decisions?
- What's coming up that requires coordination?
- What risks are we tracking and how are we mitigating them?

Make it a problem-solving session, not a history lesson.

Here's my structure for an effective OAC:

Quick status recap (10 minutes): Hit the highlights only. Are we on schedule? On budget? Any safety incidents? If everything's fine, this takes two minutes. If there's an issue, you acknowledge it and say you'll address it in the problem-solving section.

Look-ahead review (15 minutes): What's happening in the next two weeks? What activities are starting? What deliverables are due? What inspections are scheduled? This is where you catch coordination issues before they become problems.

Decision items (20 minutes): This is the meat of the meeting. What decisions are we waiting on? Who needs to make them? By when? Document the decisions made and the action items assigned.

Risk discussion (10 minutes): What could go wrong in the next period? What are we doing about it? This is proactive problem-solving, not hand-wringing.

Parking lot (5 minutes): Important topics that came up but don't need full discussion now. Capture them, assign someone to follow up offline, and move on.

Total time: 60 minutes max. If you can't cover what you need in an hour, you're either having the wrong conversations or you need to break topics into separate meetings.

The key to a good OAC is discipline. Start on time. End on time. Stay on agenda. If someone tries to solve a detailed technical problem in the meeting, stop them—that's a parking lot item that two people can resolve offline.

Your goal is to make the OAC meeting valuable enough that people actually want to attend, not just another obligation they suffer through.

Supply Chain Management Realities

This applies to everyone—contractors ordering materials and owners managing budgets and schedules.

The world has changed. You can't just assume that a generator, air handler, or specialized medical equipment will show up when you need it.

Lead times that used to be 12-16 weeks are now 40-52 weeks or longer for critical equipment. Global supply chains are fragile. Manufacturing capacity is constrained. Shipping is unpredictable.

This means ordering critical equipment is now one of the very *first* things you do on a project—sometimes even before the design is finished.

This is the new reality. You need to identify long-lead items during schematic design and start getting pricing and lead time information immediately. For major equipment, you might need to place orders during design development with the understanding that minor modifications might be needed as design is finalized.

This creates coordination challenges. You're ordering equipment before you have final drawings. You're committing to a budget before you have final pricing. You're locking in decisions earlier than anyone is comfortable with.

But the alternative is worse: discovering during construction that the critical piece of equipment you need won't arrive for another *year*, blowing your entire schedule *and* budget.

Key strategies for managing supply chain risk:

Early identification: During precon, create a list of every piece of equipment with lead times over 16 weeks. Update it regularly as you learn more.

Vendor engagement: Talk to suppliers early. Get real lead times, not optimistic ones. Understand their constraints.

Alternative sourcing: For critical items, identify backup suppliers or alternative products that could work if your first choice isn't available.

Procurement flexibility: Build contract language that allows early equipment procurement even while design is being finalized.

Buffer time: Add contingency to your schedule specifically for supply chain delays. Hope you don't need it, but assume you will.

Communication: Keep the owner informed about supply chain risks. Don't wait until it's a crisis to tell them that the equipment they need might not arrive on time.

The contractors and owners who are succeeding in this environment are the ones who've adapted to the new reality. They're ordering early, building in buffers, staying in constant communication with suppliers, and having backup plans ready.

The ones who are failing are still operating like it's 2019, assuming equipment will show up when the schedule says it should and then acting surprised when it doesn't.

Supply chain management used to be a back-office function. Now it's a critical success factor that requires executive-level attention throughout the project.

The Bottom Line on Construction Management

The daily work of managing construction in an occupied hospital isn't glamorous, but it's where trust gets built or destroyed. This is where the philosophy from Chapter 5 proves itself—successful routines and countless small, correct decisions compound into the outcomes everyone wants. When you handle change orders with transparency every single time, plan shutdowns with precision as standard practice, execute infection control flawlessly on every project, and run meetings that consistently solve problems instead of creating new ones, you're building a track record that proves you understand what's at stake. This is a demonstration of respect for the people who work in these buildings, and the patients whose lives depend on them. Master these fundamentals through disciplined repetition, and everything else becomes possible.

Section 7.3: The Owner's Perspective - What You Should Expect

This section shifts gears—I'm speaking directly to hospital administrators, facility managers, and anyone responsible for hiring and overseeing construction services. If you've been reading along as a contractor, stick around. Understanding what owners should expect will make you a better partner.

My goal here is to pull back the curtain on the industry and give you the questions to ask, red flags to watch for, and standards to hold your teams accountable to.

When to Hire a Program Manager (And What They Should Do)

If you're juggling more than one or two projects, or if your in-house team is already swamped keeping the hospital running, you need a program manager.

A program manager is your expert, advocate, and single point of contact who speaks both "hospital" and "construction" languages. They translate between your world and the contractor's world, catch problems before they become crises, and protect your interests throughout the entire process.

A good program manager does more than project oversight—they're strategic partners who help you make better decisions about scope, budget, schedule, and risk. They review contractor billings to make sure you're not overpaying. They vet change orders to separate legitimate costs from padding. They coordinate between multiple projects to prevent conflicts. They ensure your design team and contractors are actually collaborating instead of just coexisting.

Most importantly, they give you honest assessments of the process, even when the news isn't what you want to hear.

Here's when you absolutely need one:

- You're managing a capital program with multiple simultaneous projects.
- You're undertaking a project over $10 million.
- Your facilities team is already stretched thin with operations and maintenance.
- You're entering a complex renovation in occupied space.
- You don't have in-house construction expertise.

Here's when you might not need one:

- You have a single, straightforward project under $5 million.

- You have experienced in-house staff with capacity to manage it.

- The project is simple enough that direct contractor oversight is sufficient.

The cost of a good program manager—typically 2-5 percent of construction costs—pays for itself many times over through avoided mistakes, better contractor performance, and faster project delivery.

The key is finding the *right* program manager. Make sure you hire someone with actual healthcare construction experience, who understands infection control, phasing in occupied facilities, and the impact construction will have on patient care. Hire someone who will challenge contractors when needed, but who also knows when to let good people do good work.

How to Interview and Select General Contractors

Anyone will ask a GC to talk about their last five projects. Ask them about their last five *problems*. How did they handle them? What went wrong, and what did they learn?

The contractors who give you polished answers about how everything always goes perfectly are either lying or they haven't done enough work to encounter real challenges. The ones who can articulate specific problems, what they learned, and how they've changed their approach based on those lessons are the ones you want.

Here's what else to ask:

"Who will actually be managing this project day-to-day?" Don't accept vague answers. Get names. Then insist on meeting those specific people, not just the business development team selling you the work. The superintendent who'll be on your site every day matters far more than the company president who'll show up once for the groundbreaking photo.

This connects to what I talked about in Chapter 4 about vetting design teams. You're not just hiring a company, you're hiring specific people. The firm might have impressive credentials, but if they're putting their B-team on your project, those credentials don't matter.

"What's your approach to infection control and work in occupied facilities?" Their answer should be detailed and specific. They should talk about ICRA protocols, barrier construction, negative air pressure, and coordination with medical staff. If they treat it as an afterthought, that's a red flag.

"Walk me through how you handled a recent shutdown or major utility disruption." Listen for evidence of planning, coordination with hospital staff, contingency planning, and understanding of the stakes. If they can't give you specific examples, they probably don't have the experience you need.

"How do you handle change orders?" You want transparency here. Contractors who provide detailed backup documentation, explain their pricing clearly, and can distinguish between owner-caused changes and their own scope gaps are the professionals you are looking for. Contractors who get defensive or evasive about pricing are trouble.

"Can I talk to the hospital where you just finished a project?" Contractors will always have a curated list of references to share, but you want to ask if you can get the contact information for the actual last project they completed. Talk to the facilities director, as well as the project executive who hired them. Ask specific questions: Did the team who sold the work actually do the work? How did they handle problems? Would you hire them again?

It's important to remember that we are talking about value, not just price. The lowest bid is almost never the best value. You're looking for the right combination of experience, approach, team quality, *and* price. A contractor who comes in 15 percent lower than everyone else either missed something big or is planning to make it back on change orders.

Trust your gut on cultural fit too. Healthcare construction requires contractors who genuinely respect the hospital environment and understand they're guests in a space where patient care is the priority. If they seem impatient with hospital protocols or dismissive of operational concerns during the interview, that attitude will only get worse during construction.

BIM: What It Is, When It's Worth the Investment

Once you have your team in place, it's important to get everyone on the same page, even when that page is digital. BIM—Building Information Modeling—is a 3D digital model of your building that includes all the pipes, ducts, wires, and structural elements. It lets you find conflicts and clashes on a computer screen where they're free to fix, instead of in the field where they cost a fortune.

For complex renovations or new construction, BIM is worth every penny. That is, if you use it correctly—during the design development stage, and before the contractor submits a Guaranteed Maximum Price.

Your design team creates the BIM model as they develop the design. The mechanical, electrical, and plumbing engineers coordinate their systems in the model. The contractor reviews it during preconstruction and identifies any constructability issues or conflicts. You find and resolve problems while they're still just pixels on a screen.

Things often go wrong when the contractor sells you BIM services late in the process, after design is essentially complete and the GMP is set. At that point, all you've accomplished is paying the contractor to find change orders. Every clash they discover in the model becomes a change order because the design is already locked in. You're not saving money—you're just documenting how much extra you're going to pay.

That's not BIM's fault—that's misuse of a valuable tool.

The other way BIM gets misused is as an excuse for delay. I've heard contractors say "we can't move forward until the BIM model is complete." That's bullshit. BIM is a tool that's optional, not a requirement. Maintaining your schedule is not optional; it is imperative to start the job without feeling like you're already behind. If BIM is slowing down your project without delivering proportional value, you have the wrong contractor or the wrong application of the technology.

Here's when BIM is worth it:

- Complex MEP coordination in tight spaces (like a renovated mechanical room).

- Major hospital additions or new construction.

- Projects with significant prefabrication requirements.

- Renovations affecting multiple floors with vertical coordination challenges.

Here's when BIM is overkill:

- Simple office renovations.

- Projects with minimal MEP complexity.

- Small-scale upgrades where coordination is straightforward.

- Situations where the BIM cost exceeds the likely savings.

If you're going to use BIM, make it a requirement from the beginning. Include it in your design contract. Require coordination during design development. Make clash detection part of the preconstruction process. Used correctly, BIM saves money and improves quality. Used incorrectly, it's just an expensive way to generate change orders.

What Owners Should Look For in Schedules

A pretty schedule can hide a million sins. Don't just look at the end date. That's the least useful piece of information on the whole document.

Ask to see the "critical path"—the sequence of tasks that determines your finish date. That's the spine of the project. Everything else is secondary. If activities on the critical path slip, your whole project slips. Activities not on the critical path have "float" or "slack time" meaning they can slide a bit without affecting the overall completion date.

Understanding the critical path tells you where to focus your attention. If the electrical rough-in is on the critical path, that's where delays will hurt you. If the painting is off the critical path with two weeks of float, a few days delay there won't affect your substantial completion date.

Here's what else to look for:

Owner-controlled activities and their durations. Contractors often pad time for activities you control—like providing design decisions, reviewing submittals, or coordinating access—then use that buffer to hide their own delays later. If the schedule shows four weeks for you to review and approve a simple submittal when the industry standard is two weeks, that's suspicious.

Pay particular attention to:

- Design review and approval periods.
- Decision-making timeframes.
- Access coordination windows.
- Permit approval durations.
- Final inspections durations.

If these seem unreasonably long, push back. The contractor might be building in a contingency they plan to use elsewhere.

Realistic activity durations. A 10,000 square foot floor renovation scheduled for two weeks is either a miracle or a fantasy. Ask the contractor to explain how they arrived at key durations. For major activities, they should be able to show you the crew size, productivity rates, and logic behind the timeline.

Logical sequencing. Does the schedule show drywall starting before the electrical rough-in is complete? That's a problem. Do inspections happen before the work they're inspecting is finished? Red flag. The schedule should tell a coherent story of how the work will actually happen.

Milestones that matter to you. Make sure the schedule includes the dates you care about—not just substantial completion, but interim milestones like "North wing ready for medical equipment installation" or "Generator tied into emergency power system." If your schedule doesn't track what matters to your operations, it's not serving you. Remember, you need to focus on every step to clear each hurdle, so you can't get fixated on the finish line.

Update frequency and responsibility. Who updates the schedule, and how often? Monthly updates are standard, but complex projects might need weekly or even daily updates during critical phases. Make sure your contract specifies this clearly.

A schedule is only as good as the discipline around maintaining it. A beautiful baseline schedule that never gets updated is worthless. Insist on regular updates, review them carefully, and hold your contractor accountable to the logic they sold you.

Who Should Handle Your Estimates

Get estimates from people who actually build things.

A dedicated estimating firm can be good—they bring specialized expertise and independence—but getting a trusted general contractor to provide preconstruction estimating services is often better. They know current labor and material costs because they're buying them every day. They understand local market conditions. They can tell you not just what something costs, but how long it will take and what could go wrong.

The only time I suggest using third-party estimators is very early on at the programming stage when you're trying to establish a rough order of magnitude, or when you need a baseline check number while reviewing a GMP. But the problem with third-party estimators is they're typically very conservative, because they don't know your facility and aren't familiar with your team or the specific challenges of your project.

One area where they're especially conservative is general conditions—the project management and supervision costs. I've seen third-party estimates that assume a large, complex hospital project only needs a half-time project manager, one project engineer, and one full-time superintendent. In reality, you probably need two full-time project managers, four project engineers, a superintendent, and two very experienced general foremen to properly manage that scope of work in an occupied facility.

That's the difference an experienced contractor who knows your facility brings to the table—much more accurate numbers based on actual experience with healthcare construction complexities.

In reality, what matters more than who does the estimate is the level of detail and the assumptions behind it.

An estimate based on 30 percent design documents will have a different accuracy range than one based on 90 percent documents. A schematic-level estimate might be ±20-30 percent accurate. Design development might get you to ±10-15 percent. Construction documents should be ±5-10 percent.

Make sure you understand:

- What level of design the estimate is based on.

- What's included and what's excluded.

- What assumptions were made about phasing, access, working hours, infection control requirements.

- What assumptions were made about General Conditions (site supervision and management).

- What contingency is built in and for what risks.

- What the estimate doesn't include (FF&E, owner-provided equipment, permit fees, etc.).

An estimate full of "allowances" is a big red flag. An allowance is when the estimator says, "we don't know what this will cost, so we're just putting in a placeholder number." One or two allowances for truly unknown conditions is reasonable. but when half your estimate is allowances, you have a guess, not an estimate. Push back and demand real numbers based on actual design information, or get them to acknowledge that you need to advance the design further before they can give you a meaningful cost estimate.

The worst estimates are the ones that give you a precise number with no context. "$4.2 million" means nothing without understanding the basis of the estimate, the inclusions and exclusions, and the confidence level.

Get multiple estimates if you can, especially for major projects. But don't just average them—understand why they differ. One estimator might have included something the others missed. One might have more accurate labor costs. One might understand the complexities of working in an occupied facility better than the others.

Again, the goal isn't to find the lowest number, it's to find the most accurate understanding of what your project will actually cost.

The Consultant's Role

A good consultant is your insurance policy. They're the outside expert who can validate what your team is telling you and raise questions you might not think to ask. They should be challenging your team in a productive way to ensure you're making the best decisions.

Here's what a consultant should do:

Provide specialized expertise your team doesn't have. Maybe you need infection control expertise for a major renovation near immunocompromised patients. Maybe you need commissioning expertise for complex MEP systems. Maybe you need someone who understands the latest seismic requirements. Consultants fill the gaps in your in-house capabilities.

Offer an objective third-party perspective. Your team has relationships and history with contractors and design teams. Sometimes that's valuable institutional knowledge. Sometimes it creates blind spots. A good consultant can say, "I know you've always done it this way, but here's why that might not work for this project" without the political baggage.

Challenge assumptions productively. When your architect says the project needs a certain system, a good consultant asks "Why? What are the alternatives? What are the trade-offs?" When your contractor says something can't be done, a consultant should push back: "I've seen this done successfully elsewhere—help me understand what's different here."

Validate recommendations. Before you commit to a major decision— selecting a delivery method, approving a large change order, accepting a schedule revision—your consultant should review it independently and tell you if it makes sense.

Here's what a consultant should *not* do:

Make decisions for you. They advise. You decide. A consultant who tries to take over decision-making authority isn't helping—they're creating confusion about who's actually in charge.

Create unnecessary work to justify their fees. Good consultants make your life easier, not harder. If they're generating reports nobody reads or requiring meetings that don't add value, that's a problem.

Become another layer of bureaucracy. The consultant should streamline communication and decision-making, not create another approval hurdle for everything.

The best consultant relationships are ones where you barely notice they're there—until you need them. They're in the background, monitoring, validating, catching issues early, and only stepping forward when their expertise or perspective is needed.

Like a program manager, the cost of a good consultant pays for itself through better decisions, avoided mistakes, and improved project outcomes.

The Bottom Line for Owners

You're not expected to be construction experts—that's why you hire professionals. But you should expect transparency, clear communication, and teams that respect your mission. Know when to bring in a program manager or consultant to protect your interests. Ask tough questions during contractor selection and don't just default to the low bid. Understand what BIM can and can't do for you. Learn to read schedules beyond just the end date. Get estimates from people who actually build things and understand the assumptions behind the numbers. This is how you ensure your capital investment serves your patients and staff for decades to come.

Section 7.4: Tools and Resources

This is your go-bag—the practical tools that make everything else in this chapter actually work.

I've compiled comprehensive checklists for managing complex hospital projects, decoded the acronyms that fill our industry conversations, and provided guidance on using modern AI tools effectively. Rather than interrupt the flow of this chapter with dozens of pages of reference material, I've placed all of these resources in Appendix A at the end of the book.

You'll find:

- Essential Checklists: Complete project management checklists for both contractors and owner's representatives, covering every phase from construction documents through closeout

- Common Acronyms Decoded: Healthcare and construction terminology translated into plain English

- AI Tools for Modern Project Management: How artificial intelligence is transforming construction management and where it still can't replace human judgment

These are living documents that you can reference throughout your projects, photocopy for your team, or adapt to your specific needs. Think of them as your field reference guide—the practical complement to the philosophical framework we've been building.

Why Being On-Site Still Matters

With all this technology, it's tempting to manage from an office. Don't.

You build trust over a breakfast burrito at the food truck, not over Zoom. You find problems by walking the job with your boots on, not by looking at drone footage. You understand what's really happening by talking to the foreman who's installing the work, not by reviewing their daily report three days later.

The real work still happens in the field. The decisions that matter get made when you're standing in front of the actual problem, not when you're reviewing photos of it later. The relationships that carry you through crises get built in person, not through emails.

Technology is a tool that makes you more effective when you're doing the work right. It's not a replacement for doing the work.

Show up. Walk the site. Talk to people. Be present. That's where the real work of construction management happens.

Everything else is just documentation.

Closing

These aren't just technical skills; they're the nuts and bolts of the principles we've been talking about. Running a good meeting is a form of respect. A thorough MOP is how you protect patients. Transparent change orders are how you build trust. Showing up on site every day is how you prove you care about the mission, not just the contract.

This is how you build the people who build hospitals.

The fundamentals in this chapter—from precon planning to infection control to reading a schedule—might not be glamorous, but they're where the philosophy meets the pavement. When you master these basics through disciplined repetition, when you make them routine instead of occasional, that's when trust compounds, relationships deepen, and projects succeed in ways that matter beyond just finishing on time and on budget.

Now that we've covered the foundation—how to build your internal team, your external partnerships, and manage the daily rhythm of a project—it's time to look at how you scale it. How do you take these principles and lead a project, or an entire program? How do you multiply your impact beyond what you can personally touch? How do you build a legacy that outlasts any single building?

That's where we're going next.

CHAPTER 8

SCALING YOUR APPROACH

From One Project to a Legacy

We've covered a lot of ground. We've talked about the mindset of a partner, the mechanics of trust, how to build your internal and external teams, and the daily nuts and bolts that get the job done. If you master all that, you can run a damn good project.

But what happens when you're responsible for ten projects? Or an entire hospital's capital program? You can't be everywhere at once.

This chapter isn't about working harder—it's about working differently. It's about taking the principles we've discussed and building systems that scale, developing people who can lead without you, and creating an impact that lasts long after you've left the job site.

This is how you move from building projects to building a legacy.

When Your Philosophy Starts Walking on Its Own

About six months after the pediatric ER project wrapped, I was walking a job site for a completely different project, with a totally different team. I was there checking on something unrelated when I overheard a superintendent—not one of my direct reports and someone I'd met maybe twice—talking to a foreman about a complex infection-control-barrier problem.

The foreman was complaining about the extra work. "This is going to add two days to our schedule. We're already behind on this floor."

The superintendent just looked at him and said, "Look, I get it. But there are patients right on the other side of that wall. We do this right."

He said it like it was the most obvious thing in the world. No reference to me, no reference to the pediatric ER project where Matt had used that phrase to unite our team. Just a simple statement of priority that was a part of how people thought about their work.

That's when I knew. It wasn't my philosophy anymore. It wasn't Matt's either. It was becoming *our* philosophy. It had started to spread on its own.

That's the ripple effect, and it's the most powerful thing you can create in this business.

The Hard Truth About Influence

You think you're just running one project, but everyone is watching.

The subcontractors on your job are also working on three other jobs in the same hospital. The facilities staff you coordinate with talk to their counterparts across campus. The nurses you protected during a shutdown tell other nurses how you handled it. The young project engineer you mentored moves to a different company and takes your approach with them.

Your project is never just your project. It's a live-action advertisement for your way of doing things.

What are you advertising? Chaos and excuses, or discipline and partnership?

Every time you handle a change order with transparency, you're teaching someone watching that being transparent is standard operating procedure. Every time you bring someone bad news early with solutions, you're modeling what accountability looks like. Every time you protect patient care over project convenience, you're demonstrating what the real priorities are.

Every time you take shortcuts, make excuses, or treat people like obstacles, you're teaching that too.

The ripple effect works whether you are making good decisions or bad—whether you are thinking about the team, or yourself. .

From Crisis to System-Wide Change

The falling conduit incident was the worst day of my tenure as Director of Construction at the academic medical center. But something happened after we got through the crisis and rebuilt trust: The safety protocols we created didn't just fix *our* project, they became the new standard for *every* contractor at that institution.

The overhead work procedures, secondary verification systems, enhanced supervision requirements; all of it became part of the safety standard. When new contractors came in to bid future projects, these requirements were part of the baseline expectations.

Your biggest problems, when solved correctly, become your most powerful tools for creating system-wide change. The key is how you respond. If you cover it up, minimize it, or just patch the immediate problem, you've wasted a learning experience—for you, and others on your team—that comes from handling a crisis. If you dig deep, find the root causes, implement real solutions, and share those lessons with others, you've turned a failure into a foundation for improvement.

The Power of Stories

When you finish a project well, the building isn't the only thing you leave behind. You leave behind stories.

The story of how the team pulled together on the Cyberknife project to finish two weeks early. The story of how the shutdowns were handled flawlessly despite enormous complexity. The story of how a crisis was managed with integrity and transparency.

These stories get told in the break rooms and the planning meetings. They become the new benchmark for "what good looks like."

A well-run project delivers more than a building. It delivers a new standard of expectation that influences every project that comes after it.

Take the conduit crisis from Chapter 6 as an example. Once we recovered from that terrible incident, something remarkable happened: the project went perfectly. Not just "good enough," it was actually perfect.

The recovery efforts had elevated the entire team in ways that success alone never could have. The safety procedures we'd implemented became the standard that every other project on campus was measured against. Our meetings shifted from going through the motions to genuinely productive sessions—we'd look ahead for potential issues and delays, coordinate proactively, solve problems before they became crises.

Everyone on that team knew their role and, more importantly, knew how to support everyone else. There was no more finger-pointing, no more "that's not my job," and no more protecting individual interests at the expense of the collective mission.

That good scar—the one that hurt like hell when it happened, took a long time to heal, but definitely made us stronger—created something more valuable than any successful project could have. That incident created a legacy of rigorous safety policies that protected future workers and patients, and galvanized a team that understood they were invested in something bigger than just completing a building on time and on budget. They were invested in the mission.

Years later, when contractors interviewed to work at that institution, they'd ask about our safety requirements. Instead of seeing them as burdens, experienced contractors recognized them as the mark of an organization that took the work seriously. The crisis had become a story that set expectations for everyone who came after.

That's the power of handling failure well. It creates a higher standard than success ever could.

That's the ripple effect you want to create. Not just completed buildings, but elevated expectations.

Building Systems, Not Just Buildings

The trap most successful project managers fall into is becoming indispensable.

They're the only ones who can handle the complex shutdowns, manage the difficult clients, or understand how to coordinate between medical staff and construction teams.

They think this makes them valuable. It actually makes them trapped.

If your success depends on you personally being in every important meeting, you haven't built a system, you've built a prison for yourself. And worse, you've created a single point of failure for your organization.

The goal isn't to be the hero who solves every problem, it's to build a machine that solves problems on its own.

From Personal Routine to Organizational System

My daily routine that Marcus validated over sushi—the morning job walks, persistent RFI work, attention to coordination—was a personal system. It worked for *me* on *that* project.

Scaling that means turning your personal checklists and habits into organizational processes that anyone can use.

The Internal Huddle from Chapter 3 is a perfect example. It started as something we implemented on one struggling project when I was working as a senior project manager for a general contractor. The huddle allowed us to create a disciplined approach to daily coordination and accountability. Any team can use it. You don't need me there explaining it. You just need:

- A consistent time and place.

- Clear roles for who updates what.

- A champion system for accountability.

- ☒ Forward and backward looking (what got done, what's next).

- ☒ Support identification for each task.

That's a system. Once it's documented and taught, it works without you being in the room.

Codifying Your Principles

The promise of "Say It, Do It, Prove It" from Chapter 2 isn't just a catchy-sounding philosophy. It's a process of instilling accountability that you can teach and measure.

- Say It: What specifically did you commit to?

- Do It: Execute on that commitment.

- Prove It: Close the loop by demonstrating completion.

You can build this into your project kickoffs, make it part of your weekly reporting rhythm, and even train new team members on it in their first week.

It's not dependent on someone's natural inclination toward accountability. It's a system that creates accountability through structure.

The same applies to every principle we've discussed:

The Mission Immersion Process from Chapter 4 can become standard onboarding for every new contractor or design partner. Before you just jump into the project or try to solve the problem, you have a structured process for connecting them to the hospital's purpose.

The Crisis Response Playbook from Chapter 6 shouldn't live in your head. After the falling conduit incident, we created a formal crisis response plan: Stop the work. Secure the area. Get the facts. Notify leadership with transparent information. Begin an investigation. Implement solutions. Prove change through action.

That's a system. Even if I'm not the first person on-site, the team knows the immediate steps. We don't leave crisis response to individual instinct—we have a documented process.

The Trust Ledger from Chapter 2 can become part of how you evaluate contractor performance. Are they making consistent deposits through keeping small promises? Are they handling withdrawals transparently? You can create metrics around this.

The point is to take what works and make it repeatable. Turn your instincts into instructions. Transform your personal approach into organizational muscle memory.

The Test of a Good System

How do you know if you've built a real system or just documented your personal preferences? Ask yourself if someone else can use it successfully without you coaching them.

I learned this when I had to be away during those two simultaneous shutdowns I mentioned in Chapter 3. My construction managers didn't just successfully execute the work—they did it using the same MOP structure, the same stakeholder coordination approach, the same crisis protocols we'd developed together.

They didn't need to call me for guidance because the system had answers for the questions they encountered. When a minor issue came up, the contingency plan was already documented. The decision-making framework was clear.

That's what good systems do. They capture institutional knowledge and make it accessible to everyone, not just the person who created it.

Bad systems require the original creator to interpret and explain everything. Good systems are self-evident to anyone who's been properly trained on them.

Your Real Legacy: The People You Develop

Your legacy won't be the buildings you completed. Remember, concrete cracks and systems become obsolete. Buildings get torn down or renovated all the time.

Your real legacy is the people you developed.

Are you leaving behind a team of followers who need you for every decision, or a team of leaders who can carry the principles forward without you?

The difference comes down to whether you're hoarding knowledge or transferring it. Whether you're building dependency or building capability.

The Shepherd and Janitor, Scaled

In Chapter 3, I talked about leadership being part shepherd (guiding toward the right goals) and part janitor (clearing obstacles so people can do their best work).

That works when you're directly managing a team. But scaling that approach means you have to teach your leaders how to be shepherds and janitors for *their* teams.

Your job shifts from clearing obstacles for project engineers to clearing obstacles for the project managers who are leading those engineers.

You move up a level of abstraction, so instead of solving problems directly, you're teaching others how to solve them. Instead of making decisions, you're creating frameworks that enable good decision-making.

This requires a fundamental shift in how you think about your role. You're no longer the expert who has all the answers. You're the teacher who helps others develop their own expertise.

It's harder than it sounds. There's a real temptation to just handle things yourself because you can do it faster and better. Remember though, every time you do that, you rob someone else of the opportunity to learn and grow.

The Two Shutdowns: An Investment in Leadership

When I stepped back and let those two construction managers handle those simultaneous shutdowns without me, I was making an investment.

The success of those shutdowns was great. The hospital was thrilled. We maintained our schedule. Everything worked exactly as planned. The real ROI, however, was the successful development of two leaders who now had the confidence and experience to handle anything.

They'd proven to themselves that they could manage something of that magnitude and complexity. They'd demonstrated to the hospital that they were capable partners. They'd shown their teams what good leadership looked like under pressure.

I didn't just get two well-run shutdowns. I got two future leaders who could now handle similar challenges on their own, teach others what they'd learned, and scale the approach to their own teams and projects.

That's the math of mentorship. The immediate output—the successful shutdown—is just the starting point. The compound returns come from developing people who can multiply the impact far beyond what you could accomplish alone.

A Systematic Approach to Developing Leaders

Mentorship can't be left to chance. You need a deliberate process for identifying and developing future leaders.

Step 1: Identify Potential

Look for character, not credentials. Who demonstrates the "hardworking, humble" ethos we talked about in Chapter 3? Who takes ownership without being asked? Who makes the people around them better?

Don't just promote the person with the most impressive resume or the longest tenure. Look for the project manager who stays late to help a struggling colleague. The superintendent who takes time to explain the "why" to their foremen. The person who sees problems and brings solutions, not just complaints.

Character is the foundation. Skills can be taught. Values are much harder to instill.

Step 2: Create Stretch Opportunities

Give them a challenge that's slightly beyond their current role. Don't make it something so far beyond their current skillset that they're set up to fail, but enough that they have to grow into it.

Leading a complex shutdown. Managing a high-stakes client meeting. Coordinating a difficult conversation with a subcontractor. Presenting to hospital administration.

The key is "supported independence." You're there as backup, but you give them the space to lead. You don't swoop in and take over at the first sign of difficulty. You let them struggle a bit, make some mistakes, and figure things out.

That's where real learning happens—in the uncomfortable zone between safety and panic.

Step 3: Coach the "Why"

When you're debriefing after a major event or decision, talk about what happened, but try to focus on *why* you handled it the way you did.

> "Here's why we brought the bad news to the client early instead of waiting..."

> "Here's why we listened without getting defensive in that meeting..."

> "Here's why we prioritized patient safety over the schedule impact..."

Assigning someone tasks is easy. This teaches them the philosophy and decision-making framework that underlies those tasks.

This is what separates training from mentorship. Training is "here's how to do this thing." Mentorship is "here's how to think about these situations."

Step 4: Make Them the Teacher

The final step of mentorship is when you have them teach the principles to someone newer.

When your project manager can explain the Trust Ledger to a new project engineer, you know they truly get it. When your superintendent can walk a new foreman through the Mission Immersion process, they've internalized the approach.

Teaching forces you to understand something at a deeper level. You can't just mimic—you have to genuinely comprehend the underlying logic.

You are creating the next generation of mentors, multiplying the impact exponentially.

The Obstacles You'll Face

The moment you try to scale this people-first approach, you'll run into resistance.

People are comfortable with the old way. They're used to the adversarial relationships and the transactional mindset. You're fighting against decades of industry inertia.

Let me walk you through the most common obstacles and how to overcome them.

Obstacle 1: The "Rockstar" Ego

You'll always have a "Mack". The director whose ego is threatened by collaborative approaches and who eventually gets promoted then fired after destroying the team culture?

These people see partnership and shared decision-making as weakness. They believe leadership means being the smartest person in the room and making sure everyone knows it. The idea of developing others threatens them because deep down they know their value comes from being indispensable, not from creating capable teams.

How to handle it:

Don't fight them on their terms. You can't win an ego battle with someone whose entire identity is wrapped up in being superior.

Instead, focus on results. Build a portfolio of successful projects that speak for themselves. A track record of projects that finish on time, under budget, with strong client relationships and minimal change orders is the only argument that works.

Document your approach. When your team has 30 percent fewer change orders than the hospital average, your safety record is the best in the organization, and clients specifically request your teams for future work, that's evidence that's hard to argue with.

Most importantly, protect your people from the political games. Make it clear that your team's focus is on delivering excellent work, not on navigating internal politics. Shield them from the toxicity so they can concentrate on what matters.

Obstacle 2: The Bureaucratic Wall

"That's not how we do things here."

You'll hear this constantly when trying to implement new approaches. The institutional resistance to change is powerful, especially in large organizations.

How to handle it:

Start small. Find one project, one team, and make it a model of success. Don't try to change the entire organization at once.

Use that pilot project to gather data. Track the metrics that matter: change order percentages, schedule adherence, safety incidents, client satisfaction, team retention.

Then go to leadership with concrete evidence: "On this project, using this collaborative approach, we had 30 percent fewer change orders than the hospital average. Client satisfaction scores were 25 percent higher. We finished two weeks early. Here's the data."

You can't argue with results. Start with one undeniable success, then use it as leverage to expand the approach.

The bureaucracy isn't trying to block good ideas—it's trying to protect against bad ones. Show them that your approach mitigates risk rather than increasing it, and you'll start to change minds.

Obstacle 3: The Burnout Culture

The biggest obstacle might be your own habits and the industry culture you've internalized.

The grind is a hard drug to quit. The validation that comes from being the person who works harder than everyone else, who's always available, who sacrifices everything for the project—that's addictive.

As I learned through walking pneumonia, divorce, and eventually sepsis, it's unsustainable and ultimately destructive.

How to handle it:

Lead by example with your Big Rocks from Chapter 5.

When you protect your Sundays (or whatever your sacred time is), you give your team permission to do the same. When you take a real vacation—and actually disconnect—you send the message that rest is part of the system, not a sign of weakness.

When someone on your team consistently works 60-hour weeks, don't praise their dedication. Ask what you need to do to help them fix that. Is it a workload issue? A skills gap? A process problem?

The hardest part is resisting the temptation to be the hero. When a crisis hits at 8 PM, your instinct is to personally jump in and solve it. Sometimes you have to. But ask yourself if that is something someone else on your team can handle? Is this an opportunity for them to grow?

Building sustainable excellence means creating systems and developing people so the organization doesn't depend on anyone's heroics, including yours.

The 30-60-90 Day Implementation Plan

Scaling sounds overwhelming when you think about the whole thing at once. Break it down into manageable steps.

Days 1-30: Document and Teach

Identify one process on your current project that works well and can be systemized. Maybe it's your approach to change order review, your shutdown planning checklist, or your weekly coordination rhythm.

Document it clearly enough that someone else could follow it. Include the "why" behind each step, not just the "what."

Then teach it to one person on your team or in your company. Walk them through it. Have them use it. Get their feedback on what's clear and what's confusing.

Also in these first 30 days, identify one decision you made recently and explain the "why" behind it to someone you're developing. Teach them the framework you used to reach that decision.

Days 31-60: Expand and Test

Run a Mission Immersion kickoff for your next project. Bring the design team, contractors, and key hospital staff together. Connect everyone to the purpose before diving into technical details.

Document how it went. What worked? What would you change? Turn it into a repeatable process.

Also identify one "stretch opportunity" for a promising team member. Give them something slightly beyond their current comfort zone—leading a shutdown planning session, managing a difficult client conversation, coordinating a complex sequence of work.

Support them, but don't take over. Let them lead.

Days 61-90: Share and Scale

Take one of your documented processes and share it with another team. Maybe it's a different project in your portfolio, or maybe it's another project manager in your organization.

Help them implement it. Learn from their questions and challenges. Refine the documentation based on what you learn.

By day 90, you should have:

- ☒ At least one well-documented, transferable process

- ☒ Evidence that someone besides you can successfully use it

- ☒ One person you're actively mentoring who's taken on new responsibility

- ☒ Initial metrics showing the impact of your systematic approach

That's the foundation for scaling. Once you prove the concept works, you can expand it systematically.

The Legacy Assessment Tool

How do you know if you're actually building a legacy or just running projects? Ask yourself these questions honestly:

Systems Test: "If I left my job tomorrow, what systems would still be in place?"

If the answer is "not many"—if most of what works depends on your personal involvement—you haven't scaled yet. Your expertise is trapped in your head instead of embedded in organizational processes.

People Test: "Who have I developed that could do my job?"

Who could step into your specific role and maintain the same standards and approach. If you can't name at least two people, you've been hoarding knowledge instead of transferring it.

Independence Test: "Is my team's success dependent on my presence?"

This is the hardest question because the answer that feels good (yes, they need me) is actually the wrong answer. If your team only succeeds when you're directly involved, you haven't built a sustainable operation—you've built dependency.

Impact Test: "Can I point to specific examples of my approach spreading beyond my direct control?"

Like that superintendent I overheard using "there are patients on the other side of that wall" without knowing where the phrase came from. That's evidence of a ripple effect; your philosophy walking on its own legs.

From Your First Half to Your Second

In your first half, you build your resume. You accumulate impressive projects, earn promotions, and establish a reputation. Success is measured in titles, completed buildings, and salary increases.

In your second half, you build your legacy. You develop people, create systems, elevate standards. Significance is measured in the capabilities you've transferred, the culture you've shaped, and the improvements that continue long after you're gone.

The transition isn't about age or career stage—it's about mindset. There are 30-year-olds operating in their second half, focused on developing others and creating lasting impact. There are 60-year-olds still stuck in first-half thinking, trying to prove themselves on every project.

The second half requires letting go of being the hero and accepting the slower, less visible work of being the teacher. It requires celebrating others' successes more than your own. It requires measuring impact over years and decades, not project cycles.

The thing that makes it all worthwhile is the compound interest you create.

In your first half, your impact is limited by your personal capacity. There are only so many hours in a day, so many projects you can personally touch.

In your second half, your impact multiplies through the people you develop and the systems you create. Every leader you mentor develops their own leaders. Every process you document gets used on dozens of projects. Every standard you elevate affects hundreds of future projects.

That's how you build something that lasts.

What This Actually Looks Like

I see the legacy of the approach in unexpected places now.

The safety protocols from the falling conduit crisis are still in use at that medical center, years after I left. They've been refined and improved, but the core principles remain.

The mission-first mentality from the pediatric ER project became part of how people think about the work across multiple hospitals and projects. It's now just how people approach healthcare construction.

The construction managers I developed are now running their own programs, mentoring their own teams, creating their own ripple effects.

The systems we built are being used by people I've never met on projects I'll never see.

That's legacy. The elevated standards, developed people, and cultural changes that improved how healthcare construction gets done.

A legacy isn't a list of buildings on a piece of paper. It's the people you've mentored, culture you've shaped, and systems you've built that continue to deliver excellence long after your name has been forgotten.

It's the ripple effect of doing good work with good people, over and over, until it becomes the new standard.

That's how you build the people who build hospitals.

Your Next Steps

You don't scale overnight. Start with one small step:

This Week: Identify one thing that works well on your current project. Document it clearly enough that someone else could use it. Share it with one person.

This Month: Find someone on your team ready for a stretch opportunity. Give them something slightly beyond their current role. Support them, but let them lead.

This Quarter: Take one successful approach and deliberately spread it to another project or team. Track what works and what needs refinement.

The goal isn't to transform your entire organization immediately. It's to start the ripple effect. One documented process. One developed leader. One elevated standard.

Do that consistently, and in a few years you'll look around and realize the approach has taken root in ways you never directly touched.

That's when you know you've moved from building projects to building a legacy.

CHAPTER 9

NEXT STEPS

Building Your Own Second Half

Well, we've come a long way together. I offer a sincere thank you for making it this far. We started this journey back at a small MRI project in Southern California, learning that the foundation of our work may be poured in concrete, but it's set in partnership. We talked about trust as the real currency on any job site, something you build with small, daily deposits in a ledger that never forgets. We assembled our internal team of hardworking, humble people, found a sustainable rhythm to avoid the burnout that eats good people alive, walked through the fire of a real crisis, and dug into the nuts-and-bolts skills that make it all work.

But the point of all this isn't just to give you a new playbook. It's to offer you a different way to think about your work and, if you are anything like me, your life. It's the roadmap I wish I had when I was grinding away early in my career—so focused on the next rung on the ladder that I almost missed out on everything that truly mattered. This chapter is about taking that roadmap and figuring out your own first step toward a life and career built on significance.

The Man Who Showed Me What Discipline Looks Like

I was blessed with two fathers who shaped the man I've become. My biological dad and my stepdad Les both taught me the value of hard work, though in different ways. I want to tell you about Les, because, as I look back on everything I've written in this book, I see now that he was living these principles long before I had any words for them.

Les owned a commercial drywall lath and plaster company in the Midwest. He was the kind of man who believed a handshake meant more than a contract. When I was younger, more interested in ski slopes than following his example, I didn't fully appreciate what he was building.

But now, from the perspective of my own second half, I see it clearly.

Les was disciplined in a way that bordered on obsessive. Every evening after dinner, he'd sit at the computer doing family budget tracking—meticulously, line by line. He cleaned every tool before putting it away. The job was never finished until everything was perfect. He wasn't trying to impress anyone, he just believed that's what the work deserved.

I watched him model that discipline my entire childhood. It wasn't dramatic. It was just consistent.

He was also fair—firm, but fair. Funny enough, that's how people have described me throughout my career, and I can trace it directly back to him.

There's a story about Les that captures this sentiment perfectly. One day, a somewhat disgruntled foreman left the job site early to come into his office. The foreman's intent was to get his general superintendent—an old cowboy named Herb—in a little bit of hot water by complaining about how he was being treated.

The foreman told Les, "Herb is really hard on me."

Les looked at him and said simply, "Well, I'm really hard on Herb."

That was it. No drama. No taking sides. Just the truth that leadership works both ways—if you're being held to a high standard, it's because the person above you is being held to an even higher one.

That foreman went on to become one of the company's most successful superintendents. He got the message: we all answer to someone, and the standard doesn't change based on your title.

Les also valued knowledge and the continual pursuit of it. After dinner most nights, you could find him reading for hours. He was always learning, always trying to get better at his craft and his leadership.

Around the dinner table, we'd hear about the issues he was working on, his thoughts on how to resolve them, and the people he worked with and counted on. At the time, I thought it was just making conversation. Looking back now, I realize it was an invaluable education in ethical business and relationships. He was teaching without formally teaching—just showing me what it looked like to think through problems with integrity.

What I think made Les truly successful was that he understood that taking care of people wasn't only the right thing to do, it was good business.

He had a bonus structure that was almost unheard of in the industry. Not just for project managers or executive staff, but for the high-performing drywall carpenters—the "rockers" who did the actual hanging—he set quotas for how many sheets of drywall should be hung per shift, then compensated them for every sheet that exceeded that number. He also provided bonus compensation for good safety records.

This wasn't charity. Les was smart. His offer encouraged the carpenters to excel and work hard, but to do it safely. It aligned their interests with the company's interests. It showed them that their contribution mattered, and that someone was paying attention to their daily work, not just the final product.

That's the ripple effect we talked about in Chapter 8. When you treat people with respect, reward their excellence, and show them their work matters, they carry that standard forward.

Most of all, Les found success because he truly cared. He cared about his company. He cared about his family. And even though he never called them Big Rocks, I know he had them, and he always made sure they were protected.

I remember spending hours with him at the kitchen table in middle school while he helped me with my homework. He did that because he cared, and he knew that investing in the people around him was just the right thing to do.

Les passed away right around Christmas in 2023. I miss him, but I'm thankful for the legacy he passed down to me.

When I talk about a second-half career built on significance instead of just success, I'm talking about what Les modeled his entire life. He didn't run the biggest drywall company in the country. He probably never made the industry magazines or won any prestigious awards. But decades later, the people who worked for him still remember that he was fair, he rewarded hard work, and he kept his word.

That's legacy. Most of the buildings Les worked on have been renovated beyond recognition. His legacy lies in the people he developed, the standard of integrity he modeled, the culture of fairness and discipline he created. That's what lasts.

Looking back now, I see that Les was operating in his second half for most of his career. His success wasn't measured by the size of his company or his net worth. It was measured by his reputation, the loyalty of his people, and the respect he earned through consistent, disciplined, fair leadership.

That's the foundation he laid for me. And now, in my own second half, that's the standard I'm trying to live up to. It's not about building a resume anymore, it's about building something that would make him proud. Les was always proud of my success, but it wasn't because of the impressive titles or massive projects. It was because of the man I became, the good people I helped develop, the trust I built in the industry, and, more than anything, the integrity I maintain, even when it costs me.

Simple principles, lived consistently. That's what Les taught me.

That's what a second-half career looks like.

The Philosophy is Simple, But the Work Takes Discipline

Look, none of what's in this book is rocket science.

Be honest. Keep your promises. Care about people. Treat your partners with respect. Focus on the process, not just the outcome. Build trust through small deposits. Develop your team. Protect what matters.

It's simple stuff. But simple isn't the same as easy.

The daily pressure of this industry will always push you to take the occasional shortcut, send the angry email, put the job ahead of a relationship, and work through the weekend instead of protecting your Big Rocks. The true work of a leader is making the right choice in those small, unglamorous moments, day after day.

That's where discipline lives.

You'll face those moments constantly. The client who won't notice if you pad that change order a bit. The shortcut that would save two days but compromise quality. The promise you made when things were calm that becomes inconvenient now that you're slammed.

Those moments don't feel significant when they happen, but they're actually the most important work you do. They're where you decide what kind of leader you're becoming.

Your Personal Assessment: Where Are You?

Before you can progress on this path, you have to be honest about where you are right now.

There's no judgment here. I spent most of my career firmly entrenched in the mindset that grinding away, burning myself out, and making all the mistakes I've written about in this book was what made me who I was. The goal of this isn't to make you feel bad about where you are. The goal is to help you get a clearer picture of the direction you want to go. .

Ask yourself these questions, honestly:

Focus: When you think about next week, next month, next year—what occupies your mind? Is it primarily the next project and promotion , or developing your people and building lasting systems?

Measurement: How do you evaluate whether you had a good week? Is it by the hours you worked , or by whether you protected your Big Rocks—your health, your family, your faith or personal values?

Identity: Does your team's success depend on you being the hero who solves every problem , or is your team becoming more capable and independent, handling challenges without you?

Relationships: Are you building a network of contacts who might be useful , or a community of genuine partnerships built on trust and a shared mission ?

Legacy: When you imagine people talking about you ten years after you've moved on from your current role, what do you want them to say? "That person delivered impressive projects," or, "That person made me better at what I do?"

Energy: Does your work drain you because you're constantly proving yourself, or energize you because you're making a real difference?

Response to Crisis: When things go wrong, is your first instinct to protect yourself and assign blame , or to own it transparently and focus on solutions ?

Again, there is no judgment. Just clarity.

Most of us operate in the first half for a long time before we're even aware there's another way. I certainly did. The question isn't where you've been. It's where you're going.

The First Steps: Concrete Actions to Begin

You don't transform your career overnight. You start with one small change. Don't try to boil the ocean. The compound interest of good choices works just as powerfully as the bad ones we talked about in Chapter 5.

The goal here is to build momentum, not perfection.

Pick ONE of these to focus on for the next 30 days. Just one.

To Build Partnership (Chapter 1): In your next project meeting, ask one diagnostic question instead of making a statement. Instead of, "We'll start the electrical rough-in Monday," try, "Help me understand what's most important to keep operational while we do the electrical work." Then practice the Power of the Pause. Just listen to what happens next.

To Build Trust (Chapter 2): For one week, start a simple Trust Ledger. Write down every promise you make—no matter how small. "I'll send that email by end of day." "I'll follow up on Tuesday." "I'll get you those drawings tomorrow." Track whether you kept each promise. You'll be shocked by how many small commitments you're making without even thinking about it.

To Build Your Team (Chapter 3): Schedule one recurring 15-minute daily huddle with your team. Same time, same place, same format. What got done yesterday? What needs to happen today? Who needs support? That's it. Fifteen minutes of disciplined communication will transform how your team operates.

To Build External Partnerships (Chapter 4): Invite your design team or key subcontractor for a site walk instead of sending another email about a problem. Walk it together. See what happens when you're standing in front of the actual issue instead of describing it from your desk.

To Build Sustainability (Chapter 5): Identify your three Big Rocks—the things that, if you don't have them, your life falls apart. Faith, family, health, or whatever they are for you. Then block 90 minutes on your calendar this weekend for one of them. Treat it with the same seriousness as your most important client meeting. Don't reschedule it. Don't work through it. Just protect it.

To Build Crisis Readiness (Chapter 6): Review your current project for one potential safety hazard you've been minimizing or ignoring. Don't pick the obvious ones everyone's already addressing, choose the one that makes you slightly uncomfortable when you think about it. Address it this week before it becomes an actual crisis.

To Build Efficiency (Chapter 7): Remember that technology is a tool that makes you more effective when you're doing the work right. It's not a replacement for doing the work at all. Try to find a way to use technology to free up time for what's really important. Make sure your team knows you are there for them. AI will never be able to replace a hand shake or a pat on the back. Be present. That's where the real work of construction management happens.

To Build Systems (Chapter 8): Document one thing you do well that currently lives only in your head. Your approach to reviewing change orders, your shutdown planning checklist, your method for coordinating with medical staff—whatever it is, write it down clearly enough that someone else could follow it. That's the first step toward scaling your approach beyond what you can personally touch.

Take your time going through this list. Pick one, then try another. That's how you build a second-half career; one small, correct decision at a time.

How to Measure Success Moving Forward

To build a second-half career, you have to stop using a first-half ruler.

The old metrics of success—titles, bonuses, the size of your projects—don't capture what it means to build a legacy. They measure achievement, not significance. They track what you accumulated, not what you developed in others.

It's time to measure what matters.

From Projects Completed to People Developed: How many people on your team earned new responsibilities or promotions this year because of your mentorship? How many leaders have you developed who can now run complex projects without you? That's the real measure of leadership—not how many projects you completed personally, but how many capable people you left behind.

From Problems Solved to Systems Built: How many of your key processes can now run successfully without your direct involvement? Can someone else handle the shutdown planning you used to do? Can your team coordinate with medical staff without you translating? If everything still requires you personally, you haven't built a sustainable operation—you've just made yourself indispensable, which is another way of saying trapped.

From Hours Logged to Big Rocks Protected: How consistently did you make time for your health, your family, and your personal well-being this year? Did you take real vacations? Did you show up for the people who matter most? Or did you sacrifice everything on the altar of one more project deadline? Remember: the projects will get built whether you destroy yourself or not.

From Your Success to Theirs (The Ripple Effect): Are other teams starting to adopt your methods without you teaching them directly? Are clients asking for your people by name on new projects? Are the contractors who worked with you bringing that same approach to their other jobs? That's the ripple effect—when your philosophy starts walking on its own legs. That's when you know you're building something that lasts.

From Reputation to Legacy: What would people say about you if you left tomorrow? Would they talk about the projects you delivered, or would they talk about how you developed them, trusted them, made them better at what they do?

That's the metric that matters.

The Toolkit and What Comes Next

This book gives you the philosophy—the *why* and *how* of building a second-half career. But I also wanted to give you the practical *what*—daily tools that make this real.

That's why I compiled the **CM's Toolkit** — nine practical tools built specifically for healthcare construction project managers. From daily checklists to shutdown MOPs to pay app review guides, it's everything I reach for on a real project. It's my free gift to you, and you can put it to work starting Monday morning.

You can get it at: buildingconstructionpeople.com

Tools and systems are only as good as the character of the person using them. You can have the best checklist in the world, but if you're using it to cover your ass instead of serving your mission, it's worthless. You can implement every system in this book, but if you're still grinding yourself into dust and treating people like obstacles, you're just doing first-half work more efficiently.

The tools matter. The systems matter. But they only work when they're built on the foundation we've spent this entire bookdiscussing— partnership over transactions, trust through transparency, people over projects, mission over ego, sustainable excellence over unsustainable grinding.

Get the foundation right first. Then the tools will amplify what you're already building.

Your Journey Starts With Something Small

Remember that MRI project I told you about at the start of this book? The one where Marcus took me to lunch and validated that my daily discipline was making a difference?

It all started with a breakfast burrito and a morning job walk. Nothing dramatic. Just showing up consistently, paying attention to the small stuff, building relationships with the people doing the work.

Your journey starts with something just as small.

Maybe it's asking that diagnostic question in tomorrow's meeting, starting a Trust Ledger to track your promises for a week, or blocking time this weekend for one of your Big Rocks.

Maybe it's finally documenting that process that's been living in your head.

Whatever it is, it won't feel significant when you do it. That's how all meaningful change starts—with small actions that don't look like much in the moment but compound over time into something that lasts.

Look, I've said this before but it bears repeating. The buildings we work on will be gone one day. But the people we develop, the trust we build, the standards we establish, and the culture we create—that's the foundation that outlasts any structure.

That's the real work. It's not about building hospitals, it's about building the people who build hospitals.

It's about building a career you can sustain and building a legacy that matters.

It's not easy. Simple, but not easy. But I promise you, it's worth it.

Now go build something that lasts.

TOOLS AND RESOURCES

Essential Checklists

Checklists aren't for beginners; they're for experts. Pilots use them on every flight because when put under pressure, anyone can forget a simple step. A good pre-construction checklist or a shutdown checklist is your best friend.

Here are comprehensive checklists for a large, phased hospital renovation requiring multiple shutdowns:

CONTRACTOR PROJECT MANAGER CHECKLIST

Construction Documents Phase (Design 90-100%)

- Participate in constructability reviews with design team

- Identify long-lead equipment and materials (get preliminary pricing/lead times)

- Review infection control requirements and ICRA classifications

- Identify all required shutdowns and major utility impacts
- Develop preliminary phasing plan with hospital operations input
- Review site logistics and staging areas with facilities team
- Identify permit requirements and approval timeline
- Establish communication protocols with hospital departments
- Review contract documents for unclear scope or conflicts
- Develop preliminary schedule with major milestones
- Identify subcontractor prequalification requirements
- Review insurance and bonding requirements
- Establish document control and RFI management system

Bidding/GMP Development Phase

- Conduct mandatory pre-bid meeting and site walk
- Issue complete bid packages to qualified subcontractors (minimum 3 per trade)
- Clarify all addenda and respond to pre-bid questions
- Perform bid leveling across all trades
- Verify subcontractor licenses, insurance, and hospital experience
- Develop detailed cost estimate with clear assumptions
- Identify and quantify all allowances with justification
- Build realistic contingency based on project risks
- Develop detailed general conditions estimates (staffing, temporary facilities, etc.)
- Create baseline project schedule with critical path identified

- Document all exclusions and clarifications
- Prepare GMP package with complete backup documentation
- Present GMP to owner with transparency on all assumptions

Permitting Phase

- Submit complete permit application package
- Coordinate OSHPD submissions (if applicable in California)
- Track permit review comments and respond promptly
- Obtain fire marshal approval for phasing and life safety
- Secure all utility company approvals for shutdowns
- Obtain hospital approvals for infection control plans
- Verify all inspections are scheduled in project timeline
- Confirm permit posting requirements
- Establish inspection notification protocols

Pre-Construction Phase

- Finalize project team assignments (PM, PE, super, foremen)
- Conduct internal project kickoff with full team
- Establish job site trailer and temporary facilities
- Set up document management system (submittals, RFIs, etc.)
- Create detailed look-ahead schedules (4-week, 2-week)
- Finalize infection control barriers and negative air locations
- Conduct hospital orientation for all site personnel
- Establish badge/access control procedures
- Finalize site logistics plan (deliveries, parking, laydown)
- Order long-lead equipment and materials

- Execute all subcontractor agreements
- Establish safety program and hospital-specific protocols
- Schedule pre-construction meeting with owner and design team

Construction Phase - Ongoing

- Conduct daily coordination meetings with trade foremen
- Produce daily reports based on job walks
- Maintain and update project schedule weekly
- Process submittals with target 2-week turnaround to design team
- Track and respond to RFIs within 24 hours to design team
- Conduct weekly progress meetings with owner
- Prepare and submit monthly pay applications with accurate backup
- Review and price change orders with full transparency
- Maintain infection control barriers and negative air pressure
- Conduct daily inspections of work areas and life safety systems
- Coordinate all shutdowns per approved MOPs
- Track punch list items in real-time, don't wait for final walkthrough
- Maintain photo documentation of all phases
- Update owner on any delays or issues within 24 hours
- Coordinate material deliveries to minimize hospital disruption
- Ensure all workers comply with hospital protocols

Shutdown-Specific (For Each Major Shutdown)

- Develop detailed Method of Procedure (MOP) 6-8 weeks in advance
- Conduct circuit tracing and verification
- Identify all affected equipment and backup requirements
- Coordinate with medical staff on patient impact
- Schedule multiple stakeholder coordination meetings
- Obtain hospital approval of MOP at least 2 weeks prior
- Conduct pre-shutdown walk-through with facilities team
- Confirm backup systems are operational
- Assign specific personnel to each shutdown task
- Establish emergency contact list and escalation procedures
- Prepare contingency plans for common failure scenarios
- Conduct post-shutdown debrief and document lessons learned

Closeout Phase

- Conduct substantial completion walkthrough
- Create comprehensive punch list with ownership assignments
- Complete all punch list items with verification
- Obtain all required inspections and approvals
- Submit complete O&M manuals and as-built drawings
- Conduct equipment training for facilities staff
- Obtain certificate of occupancy
- Submit final pay application with all closeout documents
- Complete warranty documentation

- Conduct final project review meeting
- Archive all project documents per contract requirements

OWNER'S REPRESENTATIVE CHECKLIST

Construction Documents Phase (Design 90-100%)

- Review constructability with contractor and design team
- Verify infection control requirements match facility needs
- Confirm phasing plan works with operational requirements
- Review all shutdown requirements with affected departments
- Verify budget aligns with design scope
- Confirm schedule meets hospital needs and milestones
- Review long-lead equipment list and procurement timeline
- Establish project communication protocols
- Verify permitting timeline is realistic
- Review contract documents for completeness and clarity
- Identify owner-provided equipment and coordination needs
- Confirm project team has adequate healthcare experience

Bidding/GMP Development Phase

- Review bid package for completeness before release
- Participate in pre-bid meeting and site walk
- Review contractor's subcontractor prequalification process
- Verify minimum 3 qualified bids per major trade
- Review contractor's bid leveling analysis
- Evaluate GMP submission for completeness and transparency
- Verify all assumptions and exclusions are acceptable

- Review general conditions estimate for appropriate staffing
- Challenge any allowances that should have firm pricing
- Review contingency allocation and release protocol
- Verify baseline schedule is realistic and achievable
- Negotiate any GMP adjustments needed
- Recommend award or request clarifications

Permitting Phase

- Track permit submission and review process
- Coordinate hospital approvals for infection control
- Verify utility company coordination for shutdowns
- Review permit conditions and ensure compliance plan
- Confirm inspection schedule aligns with project timeline
- Verify OSHPD coordination (if applicable)

Pre-Construction Phase

- Verify contractor project team assignments meet requirements
- Review and approve site logistics plan
- Confirm infection control plan meets hospital standards
- Verify contractor insurance and bonds are in place
- Review safety program and hospital-specific training
- Establish document management and approval workflows
- Set meeting schedule (weekly progress, monthly executive)
- Review and approve baseline schedule
- Confirm long-lead equipment orders placed
- Attend pre-construction meeting and verify alignment

- Establish protocols for hospital staff communication

Construction Phase - Ongoing

- Attend weekly progress meetings and review schedule updates
- Review and document daily reports
- Review and approve/reject submittals within 1 week
- Review RFI responses for accuracy and completeness
- Review monthly pay applications before approving payment
- Verify stored materials before releasing payment
- Conduct independent site inspections weekly minimum
- Review and negotiate change orders for cost and scope validity
- Track project against budget and schedule baselines
- Monitor infection control compliance daily in occupied areas
- Verify negative air pressure maintained continuously
- Review safety reports and incident logs
- Coordinate with hospital departments on access and impact
- Maintain communication with medical staff on disruptions
- Track contractor performance issues and document
- Review quality of work against specifications
- Verify proper material storage and protection

Shutdown-Specific (For Each Major Shutdown)

- Review draft MOP with facilities and medical staff
- Verify circuit tracing accuracy with facilities team
- Coordinate with affected departments on patient impact
- Review backup system testing and verification

- Participate in stakeholder coordination meetings
- Review and approve final MOP at least 2 weeks prior
- Conduct pre-shutdown readiness verification
- Verify emergency contacts and escalation procedures
- Monitor shutdown execution and provide owner support
- Participate in post-shutdown debrief
- Document lessons learned for future shutdowns

Closeout Phase

- Conduct substantial completion inspection with contractor
- Verify punch list is comprehensive and accurate
- Track punch list completion and re-inspect work
- Review O&M manuals for completeness
- Verify as-built drawings match actual construction
- Coordinate equipment training for facilities staff
- Verify all inspections and approvals obtained
- Review certificate of occupancy and conditions
- Verify warranty documentation is complete
- Review final pay application and retainage release
- Conduct final project evaluation meeting
- Archive all project documents
- Prepare lessons learned summary for future projects

Common Acronyms Decoded

Construction and healthcare are in a competition to see who can use more confusing acronyms. Here's your cheat sheet.

Healthcare Acronyms

- **ICRA** - Infection Control Risk Assessment
- **HVAC** - Heating, Ventilation, and Air Conditioning
- **MEP** - Mechanical, Electrical, and Plumbing
- **OR** - Operating Room
- **ER/ED** - Emergency Room/Emergency Department
- **ICU** - Intensive Care Unit
- **NICU** - Neonatal Intensive Care Unit
- **PACU** - Post-Anesthesia Care Unit
- **L&D** - Labor and Delivery
- **OSHPD** - Office of Statewide Health Planning and Development (California)
- **FGI** - Facility Guidelines Institute
- **AHJ** - Authority Having Jurisdiction
- **ACH** - Air Changes per Hour
- **HEPA** - High-Efficiency Particulate Air (filter)
- **Code Blue** - Medical emergency requiring immediate response
- **NPO** - Nothing by mouth (patient fasting)
- **STAT** - Immediately (from Latin "statim")
- **WOW** - Workstation on Wheels (formerly COW - Computer on Wheels)
- **Crash Cart** - Mobile unit with emergency medical equipment
- **Isolation Room** - Room with controlled airflow for infectious patients

- **Clean Room** - Controlled environment with low contamination
- **Dirty Utility** - Room for handling contaminated materials
- **Med Room** - Medication storage and preparation area
- **Nurse Station** - Central hub for nursing staff on a floor

Construction Acronyms

- **RFI** - Request for Information
- **RFP** - Request for Proposal
- **RFQ** - Request for Qualifications
- **GMP** - Guaranteed Maximum Price
- **GC** - General Contractor
- **CM** - Construction Manager
- **PM** - Project Manager
- **PE** - Project Engineer
- **Super** - Superintendent
- **OAC** - Owner-Architect-Contractor (meeting)
- **MOP** - Method of Procedure
- **CO** - Change Order
- **PCO** - Potential Change Order
- **ASI** - Architect's Supplemental Instruction
- **T&M** - Time and Materials
- **LS** - Lump Sum
- **SOV** - Schedule of Values
- **AIA** - American Institute of Architects (also refers to their standard contract forms)

- **BIM** - Building Information Modeling
- **VE** - Value Engineering
- **O&M** - Operations and Maintenance (manuals)
- **As-Builts** - Final drawings showing actual construction
- **Submittals** - Product data and samples for approval
- **Shop Drawings** - Detailed fabrication drawings
- **Punch List** - List of incomplete or deficient items at project end
- **Substantial Completion** - When project is ready for intended use
- **Retainage** - Percentage of payment withheld until completion
- **Bonds** - Financial guarantees (performance, payment, etc.)
- **SI** - Supplemental Instruction

AI Tools for Modern Project Management

AI is a powerful tool, not a magic wand. It can help you draft reports, analyze schedules for risk, and sort through thousands of documents. But it can't walk the job and talk to a foreman. Use it to make you more efficient, not to replace your judgment.

Here's how AI is being used on projects today:

Document Analysis and Search

AI can review thousands of pages of drawings, specifications, and contract documents to find relevant information instantly. Instead of spending hours searching for that one detail buried in 300 pages of specs, AI can locate it in seconds. Some tools can even identify conflicts between different sections of contract documents.

RFI and Submittal Review

Advanced platforms can analyze an RFI, search the project documents, and suggest potential answers based on the drawings and specifications. The AI doesn't make the final decision—but it can find the relevant sections and flag potential conflicts that a human reviewer should examine. This dramatically speeds up response times while maintaining quality control.

Schedule Risk Analysis

AI can analyze project schedules to identify risks, predict likely delay scenarios, and suggest mitigation strategies. It can spot patterns that humans might miss—like a subcontractor who consistently shows activities with unrealistic durations, or sequences that create unnecessary dependencies.

Meeting Documentation

AI note-taking tools can transcribe meetings, identify action items, assign responsibilities, and generate meeting minutes automatically. This frees project managers to actually participate in meetings instead of frantically taking notes. The AI captures what was said; you provide the judgment about what it means.

Cost-Estimation Support

AI can analyze historical project data to improve estimate accuracy. It can flag line items that seem out of range compared to similar past projects, identify missing scope, and suggest appropriate contingency levels based on project risk factors.

Safety Monitoring

Computer vision AI can analyze job site photos and video to identify safety violations—workers without hard hats, unguarded fall hazards, improper scaffolding. Some systems provide real-time alerts so issues can be corrected immediately.

Quality Control

AI can compare as-built photos to design documents to verify installation matches specifications. It can identify defects in concrete pours, detect water intrusion in building envelopes, and flag work that doesn't meet quality standards.

Progress Tracking

AI-powered photo documentation tools can track construction progress automatically, comparing current conditions to the schedule and identifying areas that are behind. This provides objective data for progress reporting.

Predictive Maintenance

For building systems, AI can analyze operational data to predict when equipment is likely to fail, allowing preventive maintenance before systems go down. This is particularly valuable in hospitals where system failures directly impact patient care.

Where This Is Heading

The construction industry is moving toward AI that can:

- Generate optimized construction sequences based on constraints
- Predict labor productivity based on weather, crew composition, and project complexity
- Automatically identify and price change order impacts
- Create detailed coordination models from 2D drawings
- Provide real-time clash detection as work proceeds

But here's what AI still can't do:

- Build trust with a superintendent over breakfast
- Read body language in a tense meeting
- Understand the unspoken concerns of medical staff
- Make judgment calls that require understanding human motivations
- Walk a job site and notice the small detail that's wrong

AI is getting better every month. Use it to handle the repetitive analytical work so you can focus on the human side of construction management—the relationships, the judgment calls, the trust-building that actually determines whether projects succeed.